Called to be Friends

I shall not call you servants any more,
because a servant does not know
his master's business;
I call you friends.

John 15:15

Called to be Friends

Paula Ripple

AVE MARIA PRESS   NOTRE DAME, INDIANA

First printing, October, 1980
Fifth printing, December, 1987
65,000 copies in print

International Standard Book Number: 0-87793-211-5 (Cloth)
0-87793-212-3 (Paper)

Library of Congress Catalog Card Number: 80-67402

Printed and bound in the United States of America.

Scripture texts used in this work are taken from THE JERUSALEM BIBLE, copyright © 1966, Darton Longman and Todd, Ltd., and Doubleday and Company, Inc.

Excerpts from MARKINGS by Dag Hammarskjold, translated by Leif Sjoberg and W. H. Auden, copyright © 1964 by Alfred A. Knopf, Inc. and Faber & Faber, Ltd. Reprinted by permission of Alfred A. Knopf, Inc.

From "East Coker" in FOUR QUARTETS by T.S. Eliot, copyright © 1943 by T.S. Eliot, copyright © 1971 by Esme Valerie Eliot. Reprinted by permission of Harcourt Brace Jovanovich, Inc. and Faber and Faber, Ltd.

From THE COST OF DISCIPLESHIP, Second Edition, by Dietrich Bonhoeffer (©) SCM Press Ltd. 1959). Reprinted by permission of Macmillan Publishing Co., Inc.

Text and Cover design by Carol Robak

To all who have given me
Life
by calling me
Friend

Contents

Acknowledgments

To my parents and brothers and sisters with whom I first shared and in relation to whom I first experienced friendship.

To the members of my Franciscan community whose friendship supports and sustains me.

To Cathy Nunnelly, my friend and faithful typist, whose gifted fingers made my work easier.

To Frank Cunningham, my editor at Ave Maria Press, without whose encouragement neither *The Pain and the Possibility* nor this book would have been written.

To the Separated and Divorced Catholics throughout the United States and Canada who, over the past eight years, have deepened immeasurably my understanding of both faith and friendship.

Introduction

CHRISTIANITY is based on the two great commandments which tell us that human beings can neither live nor grow in isolation. Without God's love we cannot discover who we are. Without the love and friendship of human companions we become less than we are. Without faithful companions we risk losing not only our courage, but even our way.

Of all the gifts that God gives to sustain and nourish our lives none can equal the presence of a faithful friend. No sacrifice is too great, no personal discipline too exacting, no struggle too painful to offer in exchange for the ability to give and receive friendship. Each investment that we make in one friendship enriches every other friendship. All of human experience and all of life is somehow related to our ability to call another "friend."

What Rainer Maria Rilke says of poetry has meaning for every faithful friendship:

> For verses are not, as people imagine, simply feelings
> . . . they are experiences. For the sake of a single verse,
> one must see many cities, men, and things, one must
> know the animals, one must feel how the birds fly and
> know the gesture with which the little flowers open in
> the morning. One must be able to think back to roads
> in unknown regions, to unexpected meetings and to
> partings one had long seen coming; to days of
> childhood that are still unexplained . . . to days in
> rooms withdrawn and quiet and to mornings by the

sea, to the sea itself, to seas, to nights of travel that
rushed along on high and flew with all the stars—and it
is not yet enough if one may think of all of this . . . one
must have been beside the dying. . . . And still it is not
yet enough to have memories. One must be able to
forget them when they are many and one must have
great patience to wait until they come again. For it is
not yet the memories themselves. Not till they have
turned to flesh and blood within us, to glance and
gesture, nameless and no longer named to be
distinguished from ourselves—not till then can it happen that in a most rare hour the first word of verse
arises in their midst and goes forth from them.[1]

Friendships, like verses, are not, as people imagine, simply feelings. . . . For the sake of a single friendship (and
thus for every friendship) one must freely experience and
take responsibility for the life that comes to us only in
friendship. The price of friendship is as high as is the
beauty and goodness we find in ourselves and others when
our lives become the rich soil in which faithful friendship
can grow. It is in this same rich soil that we discover
God's love for us.

For the sake of a single friendship we risk setting out
on a journey in the hope of finding self, others and God.
There is no other way. This is the way that was shown to
us by him who was *the* Way to others and to God. We are
called to be friends.

[1] Rainer Maria Rilke, *The Notebooks of Malte Laurids Brigge* (New York:
W. W. Norton & Company, Inc. 1949).

1 Christianity: A call to friendship

> My dear people,
> since God has loved us so much,
> we too should love one another.
> No one has ever seen God;
> but as long as we love one another
> God will live in us
> and his love will be complete in us.
> *I John 4: 11-12*

IN EUGENE O'NEILL'S *Long Day's Journey into Night* there is a gripping and unsettling revelation. James Tyrone, an old actor, is speaking to his tubercular son. As he does so, Tyrone reflects on the meaning of his own life and questions his lifelong habit of miserliness. While reaching to tighten a light bulb which he had through all of his life loosened in order to save money, he speaks to himself and to his son, "What the hell was it I wanted to buy, I wonder, that was worth . . . ." He struggles, as if in search of an answer. "Well, no matter now. It's a late day for needless regret." But Tyrone, whose other son is an alcoholic and whose wife is a drug addict, does not rest well with this memory lapse. He talks on but returns again to the same thought. "No, I don't remember what the hell it was that I wanted to buy."

It is a curious thing about us human beings. We sometimes forget what we "wanted to buy." We have such good intentions and such short memories. We rapidly lose sight of goals. We are distracted and forget the direction we initially had in mind. It is not that we are bad people. It is not that we lack commitment. It is just that

we lose sight of connections. What James Tyrone struggled with in his life, we also struggle with as Christians.
Like him we lose our awareness of the connections between our vision and our actions. We forget that we cannot separate the love of God and love of neighbor. The
Gospel links the two great commandments:

> You must love the Lord our God with all your heart,
> with all your soul, and with all your mind. This is the
> greatest and the first commandment. The second
> resembles it: You must love your neighbour as yourself.
> On these two commandments hang the whole Law, and
> the Prophets also.

Matthew 22:37-40

Because we have forgotten the links that Jesus made between the love of God and the love of neighbor, because
we have tried to live them as two separate realities, we
have understood the fullness of neither. Unless we reunite
them, we cannot respond to the most fundamental call of
Christian baptism—a call to live as friends. Unless we
reunite them, we risk sacrificing one at the cost of the
other.

A few years ago I was giving a workshop at a Faith
Gathering in a large Midwestern city. I had titled my
workshop, ''Christianity: The Call to Faithful Friendship.'' As I was about to begin, I was approached by a
somewhat confused woman. She said to me, ''What place
does a workshop on friendship have at this *Faith* Gathering? Why aren't you talking to us about prayer? Why
aren't you telling us about God?''

What the woman could not know was that her questions were the introduction to my reflections on friendship. What she could not know was that my opening statement was to be, ''You may be wondering what
faithfulness to friendship has to do with faithfulness to the
Gospel. We are not accustomed to thinking about the

relationship between faithful friendship and keeping the commands of God.'' This woman, like most of us, has had more influences separating the two great commandments than she has had constructive help in linking them. Every good Christian has had forceful teaching on the doctrine that we were made for heaven and that we are just biding time here on earth. We learned that the best love was the love of God and that human love was somehow dangerous and should be entered into only if we were sure that there would be no mistakes. We have sometimes had subtle invitations to feel guilty if we loved someone ''too much.''

On other occasions I have heard people approach this question from the opposite perspective. Their question is like that of a young man at a retreat weekend who said to me, ''I don't think about God. I believe that if I just love my friends my life will be complete.''

Like the old actor in O'Neill's play, we have forgotten. We have listened to Jesus' words, we have set out on our journey in faith with great commitment, but we have forgotten what it is that underlies the message of all the Gospels. We have lost the vital bond linking the two great commandments.

WHAT HAPPENS WHEN WE SEPARATE THE TWO GREAT COMMANDMENTS?

Words about linking the love of God and neighbor may come easily to us. But saying the right words in the right order is not what is most important. What is important is that our lives will be radically different only if we have inner convictions about the interrelationship of the love of God, others and self. It is not a question of individual actions but of the basic framework out of which we live. It is not a question of greater or lesser but of an environment in which love is not compartmentalized. Love is not different realities as it is applied to self, others or God.

T. S. Eliot in his "Choruses from the Rock" says: "What life have you if not life together? There is no life that is not lived in community, and no community not lived in praise of God." W. H. Auden says simply, "Love each other or die." The wisdom of Eliot and Auden is reflected in the words of the documents of the Second Vatican Council:

> God did not create men and women for life in isolation, but for the formation of social unity. So also "it has pleased God to make men and women holy and save them not merely as individuals, without any mutual bonds, but by making them into a single people, a people which acknowledges him in truth and serves him in holiness." So from the beginning of salvation history he has chosen men and women not just as individuals but as members of a certain community. . . . This communitarian character is developed and consummated in the work of Jesus Christ. For the very Word made flesh willed to share in the human fellowship.[1]

In those deep and often subconscious places where we live our lives, most of us still struggle with the relationship between the two great commandments. We either carry an inner conviction that the love of God is the real love and that human love is a somewhat suspect fabrication or we reduce all love to human love. We must not keep one command at the cost of the other. The forceful words of John remind us again of the bond between the love of God and neighbor:

> Anyone who says, "I love God,"
> and hates his brother,
> is a liar,
> since a man who does not love the brother that he can see
> cannot love God, whom he has never seen.

[1] *Gaudium et Spes, Section 32.*

So this is the commandment that he has given us,
that anyone who loves God must also love his brother.

I John 4: 20-21

Sometimes we can grasp the importance of these words of Jesus only when we witness the destructiveness of their separation. I am thinking of a beautiful young woman named Jan—someone I knew for several years.

Jan was a searcher. She had some wonderful insights into the meaning and goodness of life. Though her life was neither happy nor easy, she continued to believe in the goodness of life and in her own need for friends.

My relationship with Jan was sometimes painful. She found it very difficult to accept love. She questioned why anyone cared for her. In her times of need, she became manipulative. Sometimes she left notes that said, "I know that you don't really want to be my friend." Even as she continued her quest for life she fell back into the old destructive patterns of isolation and distrust.

One Christmas, after I had known Jan for three years, she gave me a card on which she had written the following:

> I looked for a card with someone else's message,
> but I decided to try my own.
>
> It all started a year ago when
> you put out your hand
> and I could only stand back from you.
> Your heart and hand were open
> but mine were closed.
> You offered love to me
> but I would not come near.
> My cage was locked
> and you were blocked from me.
> I looked out from within
> I tried to say to you
> "You can come in."

But the words were never said.
Somehow you sensed my fear.
The nearer you came to me
the weaker my own cage became.
Then one day I began to trust
and I cast aside my cage.
Fear filled me
but it disappeared when you came near.
You brought me to life
and I have begun to find strength in myself.
Though I walk with fear and mistrust still,
though my cage can only be opened from within,
I know that you will help me.
I'll fail myself and you
but each time I'll grow a little stronger
with your supporting hand.
For I have found that friendship and love
give me the strength to accept your love and God's
when darkness seems all that is near me.

Jan struggled with life more than most people do. She knew that life for her literally depended on her ability to unlock that cage, to reach out, and to accept the love of others. She knew that God's love for her and hers for him was wound into this crucial task for her, the task of unlocking that cage and never reentering it. Jan was never able to really leave her cage. Even though she had the love of many faithful friends, and even though these friends loved her enough to say the difficult words as well as the comforting ones, it never seemed to be enough. Although her friends told her of her goodness and beauty, prayed with her and shared the Bread of Life with her, she still could not accept their friendship.

Jan often spoke of God's love for her. She said that her only fear of him was her fear of his relentless invitation to let others into her life. She said that it was easier for her to love God than to love those who wanted to be her friends.

Through several years, through endless struggles with a cage she continued to carry, her friends reached out to her. In the end she grew weary of her terrifying loneliness. Despite her belief that God loved her, despite the many good people who offered her "the sturdy shelter of faithful friendship," her cage seemed safer. The more she chose isolation, the more desperate she became. I was shocked but not surprised one day when I received word that she had taken her own life. She chose the ultimate isolation of suicide. Jan did not have the inner resources to accept God's love and the love of her friends. If it seems easier to love God than others it is only because we have not let him into our life. We do not love him until we have tried to remove the "cages" that separate us from one another.

Auden was right. We love one another or we die. Not all of us choose death as dramatically as Jan did. We cut life off in small and nearly imperceptible ways. We make small choices to avoid risks. Sometimes we claim to love God while taking refuge in a distortion of the Christian tradition that would have us believe that it is more life-giving to love God than each other. We fear the cost of caring for one another and so we make of God a distant God, a God who touches us only from afar.

Auden was right. We may die unless we love God and one another. We may also die because we refuse to let God and others love us.

REUNITING THE TWO COMMANDMENTS

From our earliest childhood we have been reminded that we are made in the image and likeness of God. What does it mean for us to be made in God's image and likeness? If we could answer this question we would have an important key to our understanding of the relationship between the love of God and the love of others.

God is a community of persons. God is a relationship. In God, each member of the relationship is important to the others. Each member of that relationship is important to us. Father, Son and Spirit each bring a special dimension to the life of every person who chooses God as the environment in which to search for life. And so, at the Eucharist, we pray:

> God of love,
> bring us back to you.
> Send your Spirit to make us strong in faith
> and active in good works.
> Grant this through our Lord Jesus Christ, your Son,
> who lives and reigns with you and the Holy Spirit,
> One God, for ever and ever. Amen.
>
> *(Prayer for Thursday of the Second Week of Lent.)*

To have been created ''in the image and likeness of God'' means that, like God, we have life only insofar as we are open to life in relationships. To have been created ''in the image and likeness of God'' means that I cut off life when I seek the false security that comes from distancing myself from others. It means that I cannot approach the two great commandments as though I can accept one without the other.

Why is it so difficult for us to see that every effort to learn to love, however unsuccessful, is an act of faithfulness to God's call to love? Why are we sometimes afraid of our stumbling efforts to love one another? Why do we continually feel guilty when our best efforts to love a friend fail and hurt us and the other person?

Our call to live as friends begins at baptism. Many of us grew up with the idea that baptism removed something—sin. We now know that baptism adds something. Baptism is a sacrament of friendship. Through it we are anointed to relationship with our brothers and sisters in the Christian community. The anointing is a sign of the strength that we can receive from God and each other. When infants are anointed into the community at baptism, the entire community present there is reminded that whether or not the child will choose Christianity depends on the vitality of the faith and the quality of the love that is visible among the members.

"Community" is a much used word in our time. It is a word whose meaning is often assumed. It is a word that may actually have little relevance for us. We may wonder where it came from and what it has to do with our day-to-day life.

The word "community" is taken from the Greek word *koinonia* meaning "God-given," "God-created." God creates community by overcoming our brokenness and alienation. St. Paul says:

> . . . you were immersed in the world, without hope and without God. But now in Christ Jesus, you that used to be so far apart have been brought very close, by the blood of Christ. For he is the peace between us, and has made the two into one and broken down the barrier which used to keep them apart, actually destroying in his own person the hostility. . . . So you are no longer aliens or foreign visitors: you are citizens like all the saints, and part of God's household.
>
> *Ephesians 2: 13-14,19*

When we enter the Christian community through our baptism, it is as though God is saying, "I'll do my part, but my part will not be effective unless you do your part." God calls us to life, gives an example of the family of the three persons that are God, and promises to provide an environment of strength and healing, but the response to God's call is ours. We can ignore the call, distort it, try to make magic of it, or walk away from it. We can also listen to the call. We can try to understand and accept it.

To say that this community is "God-created" means that we come together in God's name. We come together in response to God's word. We come as followers of Jesus who promised to show us the way, the way to God and the way to be good friends to one another along the way. We come as people who have been prodded by the incessant working of God's Spirit in our lives, a Spirit that opens new doors and calls us to walk along paths of friendship that we might never have noticed for ourselves.

The Christian community is not something into which I enter on my own. It is something to which God invites me. At the same time, my response to God's call is essential to the growth and life of that community. I bring to that community the unique and beautiful gift of myself. A conviction at the heart of the Christian life is the incomprehensible realization of God's tremendous and relentless call to life. It is knowing that "God has first loved us." It is believing that my response to accept and share that love makes a difference to God, to the community to which I am called, to the relationships created in friendship, and to myself.

Some of our difficulty in understanding friendship and community grows out of our lack of understanding of the relationship of the persons in the Blessed Trinity. We have learned that the Trinity is a mystery. We defined a mystery as a truth which we cannot fully understand, but which we believe on God's word. This approach to mystery led us to the false belief that since we could not fully understand it, we need not explore it further. The mystery of the Trinity like the mystery of every human relationship is not an unknowable, incomprehensible truth, but rather a truth so profound and so knowable that we will never exhaust the possibilities of what we can come to learn about it. When I view "mystery" in this way, I realize that I learn more about it each time I reflect on its meaning, each time I try to relate its meaning to my own life. Viewed in this way, every relationship I have with family or friends can help me gain insight into the relationship of Father, Son and Spirit just as their relationship helps me understand every friendship I have.

WHO SHOWS US THE WAY TO KEEP THE TWO GREAT COMMANDMENTS UNITED?

When we struggle with the meaning of the two great commandments, when we try to make the connection between our love of others and our love for God, we need something against which to test our progress. We look for some standard that will neither change nor fail us. We look to Jesus. The words of the Gospel are clear. They are a proclamation of community. They remind us that Jesus' love for us is rooted in his relationship with the Father and the Spirit.

We need to look at the Gospels now in order to understand their meaning for us. Jesus' words are simple and direct. We complicate them when we try to go back as if we lived then instead of seeing the words of Jesus as living words which speak to us now. Jesus' words speak to our lives now as they spoke of his life then. His words call us to life *now*, remind us that friendship is at the heart of every facet of his life. Jesus shows us how to reunite the great commandments by who he is and through his relationship with the Father:

> As the Father has loved me,
> so I have loved you.
> Remain in my love. . . .
> This is my commandment:
> love one another

as I have loved you. . . .
I shall not call you servants any more. . . .
I call you friends,
because I have made known to you
everything I have learnt from my Father.

John 15: 9,12,15

It is not just an understanding of Jesus' relationship to the
Father that is important. The Gospels are the stories of
Jesus and his friends. They contain sketches of people like
ourselves, people who did want and did try to love God
and their human companions on life's journey. They contain experiences that manifest the love of God and
neighbor as united.

Jesus' call to us to "love one another as I have loved
you" carries with it certain clear implications about the
cost of loving. Warmth and tenderness were a way of life
for Jesus. He reminds us of the risk dimension of love.
Reaching out to another places us always in a position of
vulnerability, a position of possible rejection. The life of
Jesus calls for commitment. Loving is no superficial ven-
ture. The reassurance that comes to us from Jesus gives
strength. His life says to us, "I have done this and so I
know that you can do it, too."

When Jesus is invited to dinner at the house of
Simon the Pharisee, he is greeted with formality and is
seated at the table. An uninvited woman comes into the
room where they are eating. She offers to Jesus the
thoughtfulness and kindness that the host neglected. She
washes his feet and then, in an action that only em-
phasizes what Simon has not had the good manners to do,
she kisses the feet of Jesus and anoints them with costly
ointment.

Simon and the other guests notice only the bad
reputation of this woman and, inside themselves, question Jesus' association with her. Their righteousness

draws their attention away from Simon's failure to offer
Jesus the warm courtesy that would have been a part of
the welcome of any good home. Jesus senses their attitudes and speaks to them directly. "Simon, as a guest in
your home, you failed to wash my feet. You did not
anoint me. You did not greet me with a kiss. This woman
has offered me the hospitality that you failed to give. She
has shown a tenderness and warmth that were not a part
of your welcome to me. She has received forgiveness so
she knows how to love." Jesus then turns to the woman
and, having acknowledged her great and loving faith, invites her to go with his peace (Lk 7: 36-50).

When Jesus is asked, "Who is my neighbor? Who
must I love?" he tells the story of the poor man who was
attacked and beaten by robbers and then thrown into a
ditch beside the road. The people who had the reputation
for doing good passed by the poor stranger. The
Samaritan, the person who was disliked and judged by
others, not only took time to stop, but he bound the
wounds of the victim, anointed him, and then set him on
his own horse. The Samaritan took the poor man to a
place of lodging and paid for his care.

The Samaritan seemed the least likely to be a
neighbor to anyone. Because the Samaritans were hated,
this man by stopping and offering help risked the
possibility of being rejected by the Jewish victim. The
story reveals something about both the victim and the
rescuer. It reveals that when we can reach across barriers
of fear and prejudice we may discover that there is a
neighbor in every stranger (Lk 10: 29-37).

At a Camp David meeting among Jimmy Carter,
Menachem Begin, and Anwar Sadat, Begin said, "The
task of all of life is to make of every enemy a friend and of
every stranger a neighbor."

Jesus' answer to the "Who is my neighbor?" question is a story that speaks about finding love in unlikely places, places that are open to us only through the door of risking possible rejection.

Jesus tells the story of a woman who had suffered the affliction of a hemorrhage for 12 years. The woman is discouraged. She has tried every channel of help and healing that she knows. She is making a last effort to find help. She makes her way to a crowd that has gathered around Jesus. She has heard of him and believes that if she just touches his coat she will be relieved of her great burden. She touches him, she is healed and then she withdraws into the crowd. But Jesus turns and asks, "Who touched me?" The woman is hesitant, she does not step forward immediately. Finally this frightened woman faces Jesus directly.

The woman seemed to want only to be healed. Jesus healed her, but he asked more. He did not want a momentary encounter. He called her to relationship (Mk 5: 25-34).

By the qualities he evokes in the people he meets, Jesus reveals to us what lies at the heart of our love for God and each other. He reveals the qualities without which we cannot love God and others.

Jesus had a remarkable way of being a friend to every person he met. We sense in him the ability to welcome the stranger, to find the hidden gift in those others called sinners, to strengthen the ability of the loving to love more. He loved some by confronting them with the ways in which they were unloving and exploitative of others. He challenged the hypocritical in those who made it their right to judge others with constant reminders that we not only must not but cannot judge another. He found important ways to invite all to discover and cherish the loveable in themselves. No one left Jesus less than they were when they came to him. He spoke plainly and directly, but never destructively. Those who could hear Jesus' message left him with a greater love for themselves, with a clearer sense of direction for their lives, and with a renewed awareness of God's unfailing love. Those who could not hear the message left him angry and resentful yet confronted with the truth of their lives.

Jesus reassures us that every effort to love ourselves and others more faithfully, however imperfectly we are able to do this, is a response to God's call to love as he loved. It is a response to the two great commandments as they stand in relationship to one another.

Unless we listen carefully to the life of Jesus and take time to reflect on his way of being a friend to others, we may find ourselves wondering what it was that we set out to do. Like James Tyrone we may look back on confused images of the command to love, wondering what it was that Jesus had in mind.

Loving well is not just a meaningful and satisfying experience, it is not simply a way we have of sharing the unique gift that we are. It is our way to holiness.

Robert Frost said, "Earth is the right place for love. I don't know where it is likely to go better." Earth is the home God provided for us as human beings. We are called to live here, not as exiles, but as citizens whose home this is. We are called to be involved in all of human life not as spectators waiting for a "better land" but as participants who shape and give direction to the quality of our living. Too often Christians are heaven-oriented people who miss the meaning of life here.

If in the name of the holy we strive to be more than human and thus avoid the meaning of human life, we will surely become less than human. We will never discover the goodness of the life that God waits to reveal to us. The primary channel of God's revelation are the human companions to whom we give the sacred name "friend."

We cannot claim to be followers of Jesus if we are not taking seriously our responsibility to delve deeply into the meaning of friendship with all its wonder and despite its fearsome demands. When we grow weary of our some-times failing efforts to love others there is a tendency to seek escape in loving God while saying that, after all, what really matters is the first commandment. How else can we explain the ways in which religion claims to be of God while running away from the demands of human relationships?

The most difficult thing that Jesus asks of us is that we love as he loved. He demands that our words about loving God are tested in our relationships with others. Jesus did not say easily, "I call you friends." In the same way it is not easy for us to say to another person, "I am your friend."

We miss the meaning of Jesus' life. We idealize him. We find ways to distance ourselves from him. We lock him in tabernacles, imprison him in Christmas cribs. We withdraw from him, convincing ourselves that it was dif-ferent for him because, after all, he was God. When we do this, we ignore the message of the Gospels. We ignore the message that Jesus' life, like our own, was a network, sometimes simple and sometimes complex, of human relationships. The friends, the indifferent ones, the righteous ones, the hurting ones, the fearful ones, those who wanted to follow and those who refused to follow—all were a challenge to Jesus. Each was a reminder to him of the same message with which we wrestle:

> No one has ever seen God;
> but as long as we love one another,
> God will live in us
> and his love will be complete in us.
>
> *I John 4:12*

2 The Word becoming flesh: Evolving self with others

> Thomas said, "Lord, we do not know where you are going, so how can we know the way?" Jesus said,
> "I am the Way, the Truth and the Life.
> No one can come to the Father except through me."
>
> *John 14:5-6*

OVER THE CENTURIES Christians have heard that "to be a Christian is to be a pilgrim." We have heard that our searching for self, others and God constitutes a journey. Writers speak of our being "forever on the way." Jesus called himself "the Way." He spoke of his friends not as members of the Christian church but rather as "the followers of the Way."

Each person and all people collectively are on a journey. It is a journey on which all are invited to discover the goodness and meaning of life. On this journey, the obstacles overcome and the invitations to life are not ignored. Each person's journey enriches every other person's. Each person's discoveries open new possibilities for all the others.

Our lifelong efforts to come closer to God and to one another present a challenge not unlike that of backpackers who set out to reach some distant and beautiful goal. Just as discouragement, weariness, frustration, physical discomfort, hunger, fear and errors in judgment are a part of the climb, so are these phases of the climbers' experience part of the human journey.

When the backpackers reach that summit where they look out over seven lovely lakes, each tucked into its own rocky or tree-ridged setting, the experience is an occasion for excitement and joy, for the satisfaction in obstacles overcome and of a difficult trail mastered. And so it is with the human journey.

The backpackers are not an isolated example. They are a symbol for the human family as we make our journey individually and collectively.

Teilhard de Chardin often spoke of the human race as being young. He said that we may very well be the "missing links" in the evolutionary process. He said that we are the generations bridging the primitive roots of the human family, linking it to the generations that will follow.

If we look at the journey we realize that we are just beginning to understand what it means to be human. In the past 50 or 60 years, behavioral sciences have deepened our perspective of what it means to be a human person. In that process, we have learned there is much yet to be discovered about human feelings and the power of their energy. We know little of human sexuality. We have not recognized the ways in which sexuality is a part of who and what we are. Our sexuality is related to all that we do as men and women.

If we set this in the context of a human timeline, the beginning of which is the origin of the human species and the end of which is a point in time where all human beings accept, understand and cherish their humanness, then we have a reference point for reflection. If we ask ourselves, "How far along that timeline are we in relation to human feelings?" we discover that we are not very far. We also discover that the line branches in two opposite directions. So different is the way we have learned to accept and deal with feelings that men seem to be going in a direction different from women. It is, in fact, as though we have two different sets of feelings—one set acceptable for and expressed by women, another set for men. Until the so-called women's liberation movement joins with men's liberation to bring about human liberation, men and women alike will remain deprived of a full and functional set of human feelings.

If we ask where we are on that human timeline in relation to sexuality, we discover that we are yet primitives. The overemphasis on the sexual dimension of friendship is just as destructive as is its denial. Our lack of creativity in seeing the potential integrating force of sexual power enslaves us. A history of moralizing in relation to sexuality has deprived us of the ability to formulate the key questions about sexuality. Without these questions the creative energy of sexuality remains unleashed in ways destructive of true human intimacy.

The human timeline reveals a journey just beginning. It reminds us of the value of each person's commitment to the journey. It directs us back to Thomas' plea to Jesus, "Lord, how can we know the way?"

Much is yet undiscovered about the power of the human psyche and the ways in which we influence one another through this largely unexplored channel. We know little of the human subconscious and the ways in which it affects our conscious actions. Carl Jung, when speaking of dream analysis and its importance in unlocking the conscious, said "the ideas with which we deal in our apparently disciplined waking life are by no means as precise as we like to believe."

Unless we give serious thought to where we are individually and collectively, we will suffer from the paralyzing impact of unrealistic expectations and/or discouragement with our humanness. The gradual way in which we discover the goodness of the human condition is revealed in the Parable of the Mountain.

STRUGGLING WITH OUR ACCEPTANCE OF THE HUMAN
CONDITION

Human beings live in a valley. In that valley are all the
cares and joys of life. The dwellers there love and help one
another. They also hurt and sometimes harm one
another. They struggle with all the colors of the fabric of
human existence. The people in the valley grow weary of
the pain and heartache in this life. They decide to leave
the valley to climb the mountain, believing that God lives
on the mountain. After much deliberation they set out to
climb the mountain and find God. They will live on the
mountain with God—away from the cares with which
they feel burdened.

God is on the mountain looking down. God sees the
goodness and the faithfulness of the people living in the
valley. God understands their limitations and failures.
God loves them so much that he decides to go down into
the valley to live with these good people. So, as the valley
dwellers climb the mountain hoping to find God, God is
descending the mountain to live in the valley. Without
realizing it, they pass one another on the way.

When the climbers reach the summit they discover,
much to their sorrow, that God is not there. They look
down on the distant valley and are disappointed that they
have not found God.

The climbers, with sadness and disappointment at
not having found God on the mountain, discover an
unexpected gift. For the first time, they treasure the life
they had in the valley. They recognize as gifts what they
previously had viewed as limitations. They decide that
they will go back down the mountain to their home in the
valley. When they reach the village they discover, to their
joy and satisfaction, that God was always there. They find
God in that very place from which they sought to escape

the darkness and uncertainties of human life.[1]

Like the people in the parable each of us makes this journey from the valley to the mountain. We make it not once but many times during our lives. We vacillate between the realization of the goodness of the place where human life is lived and the frustration that causes us to seek to escape to the mountain. It is difficult to learn what it means to be a human being.

It has been this way from the beginning. Adam's sin was in his demand to be like God. Adam refused to accept the lot of life in the valley. Like Adam the dwellers who sought to escape to the mountain from the valley refused to deal with the realities of life. They wanted their life to be different. They sought to make it different not by an awareness of God's presence in their lives but by avoiding that presence and seeking another place in which to live.

God calls us to live a human life, a life lived with our brothers and sisters. God loves us and our life so much, believes in its goodness to the unfathomable extent of giving us Jesus, the Word made flesh, the Word who called himself the way to the Father.

Jesus was tempted by the devil to set aside his humanness, to deny its reality, and to thrust himself from the pinnacle of the temple. We mistakenly believe that we are called by God to be perfect now, rather than by living a life where we perfect our humanness gradually. We plague ourselves with unrealistic guilt and with the belief that somehow we "ought to be different." We reject the darkness and possibility for error that is a part of every life.

We are not invited to be drifters who cling to and make easy excuses for the darkness and sinfulness that hurt both us and those with whom we share life. We are

[1] John S. Dunne, *The Way of All the Earth* (New York: Macmillan, 1972), p. 14.

called to forgive ourselves, to accept the ever-present acceptance of a loving God, and to go along on the journey which is made rich and strong by our companionship with others. There is a colloquial expression that says, "You can't fight city hall." We might apply this to the story of the human journey—the Parable of the Mountain.

We might wish that God had called us to live on the mountain. We might wish that there were no darkness in that valley. We might have preferred a pain-free way of living. We might have preferred to live in future generations where there is a better-developed understanding of all the factors of the human person.

The God who calls us to life had a wisdom in the design—a wisdom that realized how the best human life could come to be. If, as St. Irenaeus said so well, "The glory of God is man fully alive," then the God who loves us knows well how to "give good gifts to us." Unless we trust these gifts we may journey from mountain to mountain looking for God and never find the goodness in ourselves. Unless we believe in ourselves we will never reach out to share life with our brothers and sisters. We may never recognize God.

Some of our crippling expectations may come from a misunderstanding of the creation story in Genesis. We thought of Adam and Eve as "perfect people." We spoke of them as people who had the "preternatural gifts." We believed that they possessed the fullness of human goodness, wisdom, sensitivity and beauty. Their sin, "original sin," resulted in the loss of these gifts and subsequent punishment for them and us. We believed we had to "start over" again to try to be human. We believed we had to rewin the gifts Adam and Eve once had.

This description of Adam and Eve is not the beginning of the human family, but, rather, according to one contemporary interpretation, it describes the human family as it can be if we are faithful to life in the valley where we and God live. The "original sin" that we inherit is our tendency to do things as Adam and Eve did them. It is in our rejection of the human in our desire to be gods. It is in our desire to escape the undesirable elements in the wide spectrum of human life. Often we look back with regret and a sense of guilt because we could not see far enough or because we failed to reflect on the meaning of the experiences along the way.

A friend once asked me, "What if I look back and know that I didn't do the best I might have done in caring for my children?" There is an element of self-destruction in that question. Any of us might look back, must look back, and come to terms with what we see now and what we did not see before. This hindsight is what Kierkegaard described when he said, "We live our lives forward, but we understand them backwards."

This way of learning is true, not only for each individual, but also for all of human history. It reminds us of the importance of remembering that all of life has three components: past, present and future. We need the past in order to give some historical perspective. We need the past to enrich the decisions we make now as well as to strengthen the goals we set for the future. Santayana says that "one who does not learn from the mistakes of the past is condemned to repeat them." The material that links past, present and future is an acceptance of myself which grows out of a personal commitment to live my life as well as I can, to take the materials of each day and fashion them into a life that I cherish.

We inherit from those who have gone before, ancestors, relatives, parents and people of other generations, the patterns of behavior that have been modeled for us. Courage is needed in order for us to be willing to break destructive patterns of behavior and to take responsibility for our decisions. This courage determines what kind of human beings we shall be.

Governments, large corporations, industry, unions, social pressure groups have a great impact on the direction of human life. We must understand the meaning of what Teilhard de Chardin put so profoundly when he said that the human species is the only species that determines and takes charge of it own evolutionary process. The human species, you and I, determines the emotional, sexual, psychic, social and religious makeup of the human person.

Overcoming our resistance to the human condition

The conversation of Thomas with Jesus, ''Lord, we do not know where we are going,'' speaks of a feeling that is familiar to every one of us. We learn a way of being human only through making decisions and taking responsibility for the outcome of those decisions.

Our lives are filled with new experiences. We are continually being called to walk a way we have never been before. The words of the ancient proverb are repeated in our lives. ''Remember, pilgrim, there is no road. The road is made by walking.''

Countless human stories reflect the uncertainty of the way for every person. The parents of a 10-year-old boy dying of cancer say with anguish, ''We didn't know what to do. We've never had to do this before. We never expected to bury one of our own children.'' When asked how it feels to be an author, the writer of a first book responded, ''I don't know. I've never been one before.'' A young mother on being handed her own baby for the first time says, "I don't know how to be a mother. This is my first baby. Help me."

Each of us can give similar examples from life. Whether or not we learn whatever it is that we need to know, whether these experiences are life-giving or life-diminishing for ourselves and others depends on a life stance that embraces the uncertainty of the way not because we love the uncertainty but because we know that a God who loves us has placed the possibility of new life in every human experience.

The past, when we take time to think about it, tells us that some of our most precious moments and our most reassuring ones have been times when friends shared with us the feeling of fear of an unknown future and allowed us to encourage and care for them. We also remember that we have felt closer to another person when we shared our own doubt and uncertainty, our fear of the unknown.

The song of the celebrant in Leonard Bernstein's *Mass* reminds us to "Sing God a simple song. Make it up as you go along." When asked where and how he lives, Jesus does not provide a manual for Christian living. He says simply, "Come and see." Walk with me, listen carefully to the message of my life. Live your life, as I lived mine, in the valley of human existence. Learn as I learned, by taking responsibility for my life, even in the face of misunderstanding and criticism.

How did Jesus not only survive the human condition but embrace it? What can we learn from him? If our message is to be more than one of futility and despair in the face of life's challenge to walk an unknown way, we must look to Jesus as our direction-finder.

Jesus accepted the human condition with all its beauty and goodness and despite its inconsistency and darkness. St. Paul says that he was like us in everything except sin. He tells us:

> In your minds you must be the same as Christ Jesus:
> His state was divine,
> yet he did not cling
> to his equality with God
> but emptied himself
> to assume the condition of a slave,
> and became human as men are.
>
> *Philippians 2:5-7*

Jesus trusted the goodness and beauty of human life in ways we sometimes are afraid to do. He trusted the wisdom of the plan of a God who fashioned human life that grows in response to the creator's ongoing call to life. Jesus was not at war inside himself—accepting his godliness and rejecting his humanness. Jesus knew that these realities could not be separated in him.

Jesus realized that he could not walk alone. Life for him and his call to us is to believe that we cannot make our human journey in isolation. His journey was made with friends and in the context of community. Always his message was of the goodness of struggling with the inevitable tension that results from human relationships.

> When the hour came he took his place at table, and the apostles with him. And he said to them, "I have longed to eat this passover with you before I suffer; because, I tell you, I shall not eat it again until it is fulfilled in the kingdom of God." . . . "You are the men who have stood by me faithfully in my trials."
>
> *Luke 22: 14-16, 28*

Like Jesus, each of us needs the journey that is ours. But we also need the life experiences of others. There is a vast reservoir of human experience to which each of us contributes and upon which we can draw. We are inspired by and receive strength from the journeys of those that have gone before just as we are sometimes influenced by the sinfulness or lack of faithfulness of others.

> How long the road is. But, for all the time the journey has already taken, how you have needed every second of it in order to learn what the road passes by.[2]

In the process of making good decisions we become more than we were. In the process of making our decisions good, we expand our life vision. When we share good decisions and decisions made good, we nourish one another with substantial food for the journey. The example of another, the knowledge of another's courage helps us to believe that, like that person, we too can overcome obstacles.

I once attended a graduation at a state hospital school. Every junior and senior high school graduate on the stage that afternoon was in a wheelchair. Joe, the young man who was valedictorian of his class, was paralyzed from the waist down following a car accident. Seeing that young man who seemed to be imprisoned in that chair was a frightening reminder to me of just how little of physical suffering I have known. The final words of Joe's valedictory will remain with me for a long time. With a forceful voice he said, "I'm madder than hell at life. But I intend to give it my best shot." Joe's courageous acceptance of the reality of his life gave no evidence of a desire to escape from the valley of his life. We suffer a paralysis far greater than his when we cripple ourselves with inner attitudes that center on our anger with human life and our refusal to accept it. That young man is a living invitation to all of us to see in every life circumstance an opportunity to look beyond the obstacle to the life that is there.

Our realization, as members of the human family,

[2] Dag Hammarskjold, *Markings* (New York: Knopf, 1964).

that we walk an unknown way is as rich in the possibility of new life as it is fraught with the fear of error. We can embrace this reality and become more human or reject it and reduce the possibilities for life.

Every person who, with courage and conviction, helps transform the life in the valley transforms life not only for self but for everyone in that valley. Every person who rejects the reality of the valley and believes the mountain is a better place misses life's opportunities not only for self but for all others.

3 Self-discovery: A key to friendship

> Do not be aftraid, for I have redeemed you;
> I have called you by your name, you are mine. . . .
> Because you are precious in my eyes,
> because you are honoured and I love you.
>
> *Isaiah 43: 1,4*

THERE IS IN US human beings a quest for knowledge. One of God's good gifts is the gift of being able to question, to search out, to look for that which we do not yet understand. We have in us an instinct that invites us to look beyond ourselves and to become more than we are. This greatly reduces the risk of our being content to be less than we are.

The quest has been the theme of ancient writings. It has portrayed for us an Odysseus, a Gilgamesh, a Narcissus. The theme of these same ancient writings is revealed in the life of Jesus Christ.

No form of human knowledge is as vital to or so much at the heart of all other discovery as is that of self-knowledge. Unless we know who we are, individually and collectively, all other knowledge risks destroying us or obscuring the best possibilities of the human person. Unless we discover who we are we will have difficulty giving and receiving friendship. It is in the sometimes pain-filled but always life-giving act of offering friendship to another that we and our friend grow in self-knowledge.

The ancient Hebrews spoke of self-discovery as "coming to know my name." For the ancients, to name someone was to know something about that person. To name someone was to stand in relationship to that person. Sarah, who conceived at a very old age, called God on his humor and named her son "Isaac," which means "laughter." Rachel named her child "son of sorrow." After her death Jacob renamed him Benjamin, "the son of my right hand." Simon is called by Jesus and his name is changed: "You are Peter and on this rock I will build my church" (Mt 16:18).

Often the name expressed the possibilities that were recognized. To be nameless was, for the Hebrews, to be worthless. To have more than one name was a sign of many recognized abilities. Jesus has many names: Marvelous, Wonderful, Counselor, Prince of Peace, Lord, the Christ, the Savior. The city of Jerusalem was called the City of Justice, the Faithful City, the City of Yahweh, the Desired One.

In a very real way, the lifelong process of gaining self-knowledge is an unfolding mystery for us of a knowledge that is complete only for God. Only God knows my name. Only God knows all my possibilities, goodness and beauty. God reveals this knowledge to me in ways that are as affirming as they are sometimes terrifying.

In the musical *Carnival* a little girl named Lili sings of the beauty and importance of discovering her name and of being in the presence of friends who cherish her name:

> I come from the town of Mira,
> beyond the bridges of St. Clair.
> I guess you've never heard of Mira,
> it's very small but still it's there.
> They have the very greenest trees,
> and skies as bright as flame,
> But what I like the best in Mira is
> Everybody knew my name.
> A room that's strange is never cozy,

A place that's strange is never sweet,
I want to have a chair that knows me
And walk a street that knows my feet.
I'm very far from Mira now
And there's no turning back.
I have to find a place,
I've got to find a place
Where everything can be the same.
A street that I can know
And places I can go
Where everybody knows my name.[1]

For us as for Lili self-discovery is a slow and gradual process. It happens best in response to the call of a loving God. It happens best when we choose to enter into the process even when we are aware of the risks involved. One of the great impediments to coming to know who we are is the fear that we may not like who we are, that others may not like who we are.

Recently I saw an ad in an airlines magazine. That ad, from the Gold Information Center, has profound implications. It read: "You will understand why gold is so precious when you know how little exists." Each of us is unique, rarer than the purest gold. Each of us is, to use Teilhard's decription of the human person, "an irreplaceably precious gift." Coming to know and believe in the gift that we are happens only in relationship. It involves, simultaneously, three dimensions: believing in ourselves, responding to God's call to discover and love ourselves, and the realization that we cannot do this in isolation from friends who affirm and challenge us—friends who *name* us and help us to discover our name.

Jesus reminds us of our responsibility to discover and share the irreplaceably precious gift we are in two short parables:

[1] David Merrick, *Carnival* (Metro-Goldwyn-Mayer, Inc. 1961).

> The kingdom of heaven is like treasure hidden in a field
> which someone has found; he hides it again, goes off
> happy, sells everything he owns and buys the field.
> Again, the kingdom of heaven is like a merchant look-
> ing for fine pearls; when he finds one of a great value
> he goes and sells everything he owns and buys it.
>
> *Matthew 13: 44-46*

Most of us grew up understanding that the treasure hidden and the pearl of great price were the gift of faith. If we
look upon these parables as Jesus' invitation to come to
know and love ourselves, they take on great significance.
They have a meaning related to the thesis that the human
self is like an iceberg. The top of the iceberg is likened to
the self-knowledge that we have. The vast unseen portion
of the iceberg is the undiscovered self that St. Paul speaks
of in Ephesians 3:15-17 "This, then, is what I pray,
kneeling before the Father . . . may he give you the power
through his Spirit for your hidden self to grow strong."

How do I discover my name? How do I discover who
I am?

The gradual discovery of self, the knowledge of self, accepting self and, finally, loving self are interrelated and
inseparable. Each step leads naturally to the next. Each is
related to our commitment to friendship.

The fear that knowing myself more may mean liking
myself less is a crippling phantom. A God who loves us
has set in each of us a vast treasure of goodness and
possibility. True knowledge of self, a realistic understanding of our gifts and limitations, can lead only toward
greater self-respect and love if we are faithful to that
which we discover.

One important aspect of discovering who we are is
related to knowing our limitations. It is related to knowing who we are not. When John the Baptist was asked,

"Who are you?" he began by some important statements of who he was not. Like John, we must be able to say who we are not.

John's response touched on his own realization that the answer to the question "Who are you?" is never finished. We are continually discovering more about ourselves as we search for the meaning of our lives and try to understand more clearly what the call to life is asking of us each day.

Like John, each of us has strengths and limitations. Even though there are, at times, an abundance of people around us who continually point out our limitations, we need to test the reality of our limitations with the perceived limitations others reflect to us. Unfortunately, because we often receive less feedback on our strengths, it may take a longer time for us to recognize or name them.

I have sometimes invited those with whom I share retreat weekends to take a piece of paper and write three personal limitations of which they are aware. The exercise is completed almost as quickly as people can write. When I ask them to write three gifts they cherish in themselves, the response is a very different one. People frown, shift positions in their chairs and, in the end, few complete the list of three gifts. What a commentary on how we relate to one another. How important are the words on the poster: "If you love someone, tell them."

John the Baptist knew who he was not and that knowledge set him free to be who he was. He made it very clear to his questioners that he was not the Messiah. He said, "I am the voice, the one preparing the way. . . ." He refused to let his disciples make of him something that he knew he was not. Because John knew who he was he dealt with their expectations of him in a straightforward manner.

John did not emulate Jesus in every way. He was his

own person. He chose a lifestyle very different from that of Jesus. Jesus' complaint to his critics gives testimony to this when he says: "For John came, neither eating nor drinking, and they say, 'He is possessed.' The Son of Man came, eating and drinking, and they say, 'Look, a glutton and a drunkard' " (Mt 11: 18-19).

Because John understood who he was not, he set himself free to be who he was. John speaks clearly: "A man can lay claim only to what is given him from heaven. You yourselves can bear me out: I said: I myself am not the Christ; I am the one who has been sent in front of him" (Jn 3:28).

Like John, we must continually seek to know more clearly who we are. When we are asked the question, "Who are you?" we may respond in a variety of ways.

Our response may be in the light of what we do. We may say, "I am a teacher, a nurse, a carpenter, a student, a truck driver, a salesclerk."

Our response may tell the inquirer how we spend our time. "I am the one who cleans the house, buys the groceries, works as a volunteer on a crisis line, staffs a hospital emergency room."

Our response to the question, "Who are you?" may be made in terms of relationships that we have. "I am a daughter, a mother, a grandfather, a husband, a neighbor, a cousin, a friend."

We may respond out of a religious orientation. "I am a Christian, a Moslem, a Buddhist, a Baptist, a Catholic."

Discovering who we are involves not only knowing who we are and who we are not, it also involves establishing some working relationship, some setting of priorities between all of our "I am" responses.

Each of us is in a variety of roles. Each of us has many different relationships and responsibilities to ourselves and others. It is the recognition of these roles and the establishing of our own sense of identity that determine who we are.

We establish our identity out of a context of ideals and values that we have as these relate to the person we would like to be. Others, in their perceptions of us, tell us who they think we are and who they wish we were.

There is also the person that we are most of the time—the person who struggles with all of these variables:

> Each man's life represents a road toward himself, an attempt at such a road, the intimation of a path. No man has ever been entirely and completely himself. Yet each one strives to become that—one in an awkward, the other in a more intelligent way, each as best he can.
> . . . We all share the same origin . . . all of us come in at the same door. But each of us strives toward his own destiny. We can understand one another; but each of us is able to interpret himself to himself alone.[2]

The way to personal identity and personal integration is a long one. It is not one journey, but many. It involves setting out again and again, in the light of personal growth and in the face of personal disappointment and failure. It asks the courage to believe in the precious gift of the yet undiscovered self. It calls for the risk of reaching out and trusting others along the way. It presupposes the acceptance of God's love and care for us.

As we make the journey, we discover that we do not name ourselves. Our name is a gift from God and others. It is only in human companionship that we discover the name that God already knows and that others help us to clarify and recognize.

God said of Jesus: "This is my Son, the Beloved. Listen to him" (Mk 9:8). When we listen to Jesus, what

[2] Herman Hesse, *Demian* (New York: Bantam Books, Inc.), Prologue.

do we discover? When we look carefully at his life, what do we observe?

Like John the Baptist, Jesus knew clearly who he was not and who he was. Jesus' disciples continually wanted to make of him an earthly king. He reminded them, "My kingdom does not belong to this world" (Jn 18:36). And when his disciples wanted him to show his leadership by earthly power, he countered with a reminder of a kind of power that is greater: "Do you not know that the kingdom is within you?" Having asked the woman at the well of Samaria for a drink of water, Jesus says:

> Whoever drinks this water
> will get thirsty again;
> but anyone who drinks the water that I shall give
> will never be thirsty again:
> the water that I shall give
> will turn into a spring inside, welling up to eternal life.
>
> *John 4:14*

Jesus spoke of who he was out of the life experience that had been challenged by bitter critics and strengthened by faithful friends. Jesus spoke of who he was out of his identity with his Father and the Spirit—his community of life and love.

Jesus says with confidence:

> I am the bread of life.
> He who comes to me will never be hungry;
> he who believes in me will never thirst.
>
> *John 6:35*

Jesus' personal conviction of who he was flowed over into the life of those who walked with him. When others find the message of Jesus too much for them, when they turn from Jesus in ways that people will when confronted with a person of integrity and conviction, Jesus turns to his friends and says to them, "What about you? Do you want to go away, too?" Peter's response is a recognition of

Jesus' faithfulness to the Father's call to life and his willingness to share that life with his friends: "Lord, who shall we go to? You have the message of eternal life" (Jn 6: 67-68).

These stories and others will not touch us unless we believe that Jesus was human, not in some romantic or idyllic way but in all the ways in which we are. Our inability to come to terms with the humanness of Jesus has blinded us to the humanizing power of the story of the ways in which Jesus was tempted. It has set us far apart from the man who was rejected by his friends and cruelly criticized by his enemies. It has allowed us some easy explanation for the prayer in the garden of Gethsemane when Jesus asks if it is possible to avoid the suffering that lies ahead. It has permitted us to deny the loneliness of Jesus on the cross when he prays, "My God, my God, why have you deserted me?" (Mt 27:47).

Because of our reluctance to make the journey in self-discovery that Jesus made and our belief that because Jesus was God it was somehow different for him, we lose our truest touchstone. We lose the reference point in relation to which we understand the meaning of God's call to discover our name as God knows it and as others will come to cherish it.

Each added understanding of self, each new gift identified, each opportunity to share who we are with others and every willingness to be open to the response of another brings us closer to knowing who we are. Each time we listen carefully and believe in God's call, we grow more secure in who we are: "Do not be afraid, I have called you by your name. You are precious in my eyes." Each time we respond to another who calls us "friend" our ability to respond to God and others is strengthened.

Jesus' life, like our own, was a faithful response to God's call to discover more fully who he was and what his life would ask of him. In the early years of Jesus' life we do not hear the clear statements of who he was and what he had come to do. Jesus' understanding of who he is is an outgrowth of the faithfulness with which he followed the Father's call and responded. His relationships with his friends and his followers revealed to him the meaning of that call and of his life. It was in the giving of who he was and in the receiving of the gifts of others that Jesus discovered the fullest understanding of his own name, a name that is above and beyond all others:

> But God raised him on high
> and gave him the name
> which is above all other names
> so that all beings
> in the heavens, on earth and in the underworld,
> should bend the knee at the name of Jesus
> and that every tongue should acclaim
> Jesus Christ as Lord,
> to the glory of God the Father.

Philippians 2:9-11

Jesus gave us the gift of himself and, by so doing, gave us also the gift of ourselves. Gift-giving, for us as for Jesus, is related to self-discovery. When we give a gift to a friend, we reveal something of ourselves in the selection we make. We also reveal what we know of our friend because of what we choose to give.

Naming is a special kind of gift-giving. The nicknames that friends give to one another reveal both the person giving the name and the one named. The tender names that lovers have for each other involve the risk of revealing something of self in the very act of saying something that one cherishes about the other. We cannot truly give a name to someone of whom we have no knowledge.

In a negative way, the uncomplimentary titles that

people use in reference to one another reveal both the person naming and the person named. The gift of this kind of naming may lie in its challenge to own the name, however painfully, or to put it aside after having looked carefully to see whether or not it says anything true about us.

In friendship we give our name, the gift of who we are to another. We can do this only as we gradually come to know more of ourselves. Is not one of the challenges that rest deep at the heart of friendship the ongoing urge to continue to discover more of who we are so that we can continually unlock the mystery of a friend by our willingness to share what we are learning about both ourselves and the friend? This is at the heart of the mutuality of friendship. In the act of sharing, we receive. By our willingness to give and receive, we become more of who we are. To use the iceberg analogy, the top of the iceberg grows more prominent and the unseen portion is reduced.

Behavioral scientists tell us that we cannot come to self-identity unless we have been affirmed. Certainly the affirmation and shared life of friends is one portion of the long personal pilgrimage in discovering who we are and believing in the person we discover. But, for us as Christians, it is important that we never forget that the one who affirms us beyond all others, the one who calls us to the possibilities that are deep inside us, who loves us when we grow and when we, in our sinfulness or personal darkness, refuse to grow, that source of life and that center of all being is the God who possesses and cherishes our name.

In being loved by God and others we are, in the words of a song, "all and more than we had ever dreamed we'd be." We are like friends we have met in stories that have touched our lives. We are like Dulcinea in the *Man from LaMancha* who was transformed from a coarse street girl into a loving woman by Quixote's belief in her. We are like the flower girl in *My Fair Lady* who is gentled by the attentiveness of Henry Higgins. We are like the crippled child who has the courage to walk because of the love of parents. We are like the Helen Kellers of the world who respond to the tough and tender love of a good teacher who sees what we do not see. We are like the woman at the well of Samaria who receives the living water and becomes not only a believer but an apostle who brings the good news of life to others.

In his poem "Build Soil," Robert Frost says, "But inside in is where we've got to get. My friends all know I'm interpersonal. But long before I'm interpersonal, Away 'way down inside I'm personal."

Are not these words of the poet one of life's greatest challenges, the challenge to reach inside to discover ourselves while at the same time reaching out to others? Do they not speak of the difficulty we have in finding some central place where we experience a creative tension that differs greatly from the "place of balance" which removes the possibility of life? We are involved in the task of finding out who we are and what it is God has locked in that treasure that is ourselves. We do this in relationship to others who know the same tension. We strive to give and receive, to see who we are and who we are not. We look beyond what we now know to what we do not yet know. We find ourselves almost always slightly outside the center where the tension remains. We give and find it difficult to receive. We rejoice in what we know and we wrestle with fears of the unknown. We fear the responsibility that follows upon knowing more about self or another.

Unless we are willing to live in the healthy tension that is a part of finding the place of life, we risk the possibility of retreating into what Christopher Lasch has called a form of pathology, the growing narcissism in individuals and in our national character. He relates this narcissism to therapies that not only encourage us to be ''our own best friend,'' but would have us believe that we can do very well if we are our only friend. He relates it to the mentality that invites us not only to do what we ought to do for ourselves, but to a kind of preoccupation with ''looking out for number one'' that allows us to treat others in a manner that shows little respect for who they are. The destruction in all this is the placing of undue emphasis on one goal so as to devalue another. Finding the treasure in the field of my own hidden self will enable me to share what I have discovered and thus make it more possible for someone else to do the same. Not only does this strengthen the one who journeys, but it makes the journey less lonely for all.

Dag Hammarskjold's words, ''The longest journey we make is the journey inward,'' are beautiful and poetic. We take them seriously and set out on that journey. When we do, we discover that this journey is made only with great personal investment. While admitting that we need human companionship on that journey we realize that, in many ways, we make it alone. With this emphasis on our need for personal relationships we have some understanding of a corporation sign that reads: ''The new frontier of the space age: INNER SPACE.'' It took our scientists and technologists a long time to develop the sophisticated equipment that put a man on the moon. The astronauts who ventured there showed a personal discipline and a grueling training that defy simple description. But, even in space travel, there are instruments that measure direction. There are indicators of how far along that journey the ship and its passengers have come. When we journey in inner space, we are in uncharted and unchartable territory. Any direction and charting remain somewhat unclear. While we make the journey we understand the importance of companionship. We understand what Gustav Thibon, a French philosopher, meant when he said that when we walk alone, we hardly know if we are climbing. But, almost infallibly, when we give our hand to someone, we immediately know the difference. There are friends in whose presence we can only climb. There are others whose influence weighs us down. It is true that, in order to know well where we are going, we must not walk alone. And, to see most clearly, we must walk with a sense of commitment and trust in the one with whom we walk.

We have had the experience of a conversation on an airplane where we were engaged, either at our initiation or someone else's, in a level of sharing that later surprised us. We wonder why it was so easy to give such confidence to a stranger. We may even be disappointed that we shared something that we have not shared with a friend. We may have put words around some experience that we have never before been able to verbalize. This is surprising only until we remember that strangers ask nothing of us. When the plane lands the sharing is finished. We walk away from that person and, most often, never see him or her again. Ongoing risk and personal involvement are seldom asked. Refreshing and helpful as such encounters may be, they are not the stuff of which continuing self-knowledge is made. Neither are they basic to the fabric of faithful friendship. It is in our ongoing commitment to frame our inner journey in words which we share in friendship that self-discovery happens and friendship deepens.

Every life experience offers the possibility either of new life or of a better understanding of present life. Crisis times carry with them new insights into ourselves but they do so at a high personal price because they open up yet undiscovered life. Who of us has not had the experience, at some turning point in our lives, of identifying feelings or of behaving in a manner that is so foreign to us as to frighten us? Do we not, at these times, ask ourselves who we really are since the person we see now was not known to us before?

People who face the grieving that results from the death of a loved one or the loss of a loved one through divorce or failed friendship are often paralyzed by their emotional states until they learn something of the nature of the grieving process. Sometimes people say, "Not only have I lost someone I love, now I am losing my mind." They discover a self in this crisis that was unknown to them. They fear the self that is revealed, a self that expresses feelings foreign to or unacceptable to their former self-image. At these times and always a God who loves us is there saying, "Do not be afraid. . . . I have called you. . . . You are precious. . . ."

One of the most frequently asked questions is, "Who are you?" We answer that question with, "I am . . ." Even when the question and the answer seem to be the same when repeated, there is a sense in which the answer to that question is never the same. We are not the same person we were several years ago—not even several weeks ago. Just as much of the physical composition of our bodies is replaced and changes, so much more do we change as the human journey we make unfolds. Each friend we have makes this same journey and so no friend remains the same.

The meaning of Lili's song cuts much deeper than her need to find new friends and familiar places in her new town. The Mira she has left is a symbol of letting go of the Lili she has been. The new town to which she goes is like the undiscovered in ourselves. Our journey, like Lili's, is a never-ending series of leaving the familiar to discover the unfamiliar, of uprooting in order to set down new and deeper roots. Our journey, like Lili's, calls us to discover who we are through recognizing the familiar and the unfamiliar in ourselves and in our friends.

Leaving Mira is a symbol of leaving the familiar and entering into the unfamiliar that is a part of every friendship as it grows and changes. Faithfulness to this symbol may even ask of us the willingness to leave one friendship and to be open to the life that can only be found in another.

Faithfulness to our lives and our awareness of the gifts that come to us only in friendship grow as God's loving call pursues us. God's gifts of courage and hope strengthen us when we fail even as they awaken in us a sense of the wonder and goodness of life. It is the gradual revelation of all that is precious in us that reminds us of God's loving words, "Do not be afraid, for I have redeemed you." It is these same words that strengthen us to say with Lili, at each turning point in our lives, "I'm very far from Mira now and there's no turning back."

4 The life stance of the listening heart

As for the part in the rich soil, this is people with a noble and
generous heart who have heard the word and take it to
themselves and yield a harvest through their perseverance.

Luke 8:15

I REMEMBER WELL one visit to the home of my youngest
brother. It was Mother's Day. The activity on that particular afternoon centered around the planting of the
family garden. Each of the six children, from the oldest to
three-year-old Katy, the youngest, had a part in the making of the garden. The plot had been a garden for several
years. The soil had been carefully tended to insure its
richness for a good harvest. The garden had been
planned, the rows established and the furrows made
ready to receive the seeds. Each of the children, except
Katy, had planted his or her choice of vegetable.

The rest of the family and I watched intently as little
Katy headed down to the corner of the yard to plant her
carrot seeds. For every carrot seed that reached the fur-
row through the efforts of her small, uncoordinated fist, at
least a dozen found a home somewhere else. The fence
around the garden, the shrubs nearby, the neighbor's
doghouse, the cat's food dish—all were the recipients of
Katy's carrot seeds. I smiled as I had a fantasy of how the
world (at least that small neighborhood) risked being
overrun with carrots.

When Katy reached the end of her row, she retraced
her steps in an effort to cover the seeds with soil. She re-
joined the family on the patio and said to her father,

"Daddy, will every one of my carrot seeds grow?" She seemed satisfied by her father's review of the best conditions for growth and the reasons why not every seed would provide a fresh carrot for the family table.

Katy's planting and her father's efforts to reduce her disappointment about the carrot yield gave me some unexpected insights into the parable of the sower when I heard it read a few days later.

THE RICH SOIL OF THE LISTENING HEART

In the parable of the sower we are introduced to a planter who, much like Katy, puts seeds in a variety of places. Some seem likely places for seeds to grow and others seem like places where the expectation of a yield is minimal. In telling us that the seeds fell in four distinct places, and that these represent four distinct kinds of people, Jesus is inviting us to listen and learn. He challenges us to a consideration of the quality of our listening. In each example we recognize symbols that illustrate for us the degree of preparedness for listening.

Jesus tells us that seeds fell on the edge of the path, on the rock, among the thorns, and in rich soil. The place at the edge of the path is like the person who stays distant from life. Such a person chooses to be uninvolved, refuses to enter into life, and fears the possible hurt of being a participant rather than a spectator. Such a person may notice life in self and others and then turn from that life because it asks too much to leave the "edge of the path" and enter in.

The place on the rock is like the person who lacks depth, the nonreflective person, the person who misses the messages that are everywhere because of a superficial, nondemanding approach to life.

The place in the thorns is like the person who complicates life by letting everything in. Such a person lacks the selectivity and inner resources needed to clarify personal values and to put aside those which are not helpful to life.

The place of the rich soil is like the person who is open and receptive to life. This person takes carefully considered risks but also takes responsibility for life's direction. This person has prepared the rich soil and has recognized the ongoing investment that must be made lest the soil lose its richness.

Jesus makes it clear that the rich soil of the human heart is linked with a difficult human commitment—the commitment to become a listener. His story points out that listening is not something we do so much as it is a way in which we live. He relates this way of living to people who have "noble and generous hearts."

Throughout the pages of Sacred Scripture there are frequent reminders that personal investment in growing to be a person who listens is a prerequisite for all who would follow God's call to life.

Roger Garaudy, a French communist who has written two books on dialogue, says that more than half of communicating is listening. He asks, "What are our reasons for wanting to communicate?" Then he describes a variety of possibilities: to convince ourselves, to convince others, to share ideas, to search with others, to share ourselves as well as our ideas. His final sentence touches on any kind of listening relationship in which we might ever be involved. He says that only insofar as our desire for communication is more than a means of persuading another to assume our way of thinking are we really faithful to communication.

We miss the message of Jesus' parable if we put the words aside with some inner decision that some people are "born listeners" and that listening comes easy to them. That is what the parable is all about. No one is a "born listener" anymore than anyone is a "born speaker" or a born Olympic speed skater. Listening, like speaking and speed skating, is demanding, asks personal discipline and a clear commitment to the goal. It demands the personal sacrifice without which one does not listen, speak or skate well.

One does not easily assume the life stance of the listener. To become a better listener asks that I notice some things about my present ways of listening. It might be helpful to take the following personal inventory:

—Who are the people I like to listen to?

There may be a variety of people to whom we enjoy listening. Generally we like to listen to those who have something to say to us. We like to listen to those who may challenge us, but people whose challenges carry with them something of value to us.

I have never believed that there are large numbers of people who listen only to those who will "tell them what they want to hear," though each of us may have fit that description at some particular time for some special reason. I believe that people who are serious about their lives will come through this destructiveness as they come to terms with their own rationalizations.

—Who are the people who are difficult for me to listen to?

If we know who these people are and have some insight as to the reason why they are hard to listen to, we already have some important keys to our own listening. Personal discomfort in this regard will tell us something that we would do well to examine carefully. We may discover that there is no basis for the discomfort. We may also discover that this person touches on something that is related closely to our own growing edges. When this is true, we have received another of life's painful gifts.

—Who is a person who listened to me at a time when it was important?

Recalling when someone listened, who that person was and why it was important will remind us not only of a special gift we received, but also of the important differences between people who show their care by listening and those who lack the patient qualities that are involved in listening. Good listeners are channels of life for us.

—When did my listening help someone?

If we can recall the circumstances, and can identify what it was that made a difference to the person we listened to, we will better understand not only what that person needed at the time, but what we may sometimes need. Recalling such an incident is an invitation to feel good about ourselves for having been a channel of life for someone else because we were able to listen.

—When did I fail to listen when someone needed me?

Looking back at times when we said we did not have time, could not be there, or were not able to listen are also important recollections. They are important not when we use them as occasions for undue guilt, but because they may reveal to us some of our fears, our tendencies toward overcommitment. The important thing to note is any pattern that may be present in our failure to listen.

Listening is not a call to be the victim of people who prefer to rehearse their lives endlessly rather than take charge of them. It is not a commitment to allow ourselves to be exploited. It is not a promise to give more than we have. It is an invitation to recognize that listening is one important way to be a friend.

—When did someone fail to listen to me when I needed to be heard?

I am convinced that human loneliness is among the most fearsome of all experiences. It is at once our call to life and our fear that this seemingly empty space is not a place of life. The place in us where we must walk alone borders a place where we must have the courage to reach out to others.

I believe that each of us has felt at some time that there was no one to listen. This may be true. It may also be true that no one listened because we did not ask them to or because we asked in such a garbled way that no hearer could understand what we said. Asking for the help we need is something that most of us do with reluctance. We have believed that "it is better to give than to receive" in such a way as to forget that one important way we give is to trust another by asking for what we need.

—How do I listen?

We need to learn that listening is not simply a matter for good hearing. It is not a matter of telling someone that we will listen. It is rather communicating an attitude that this person matters to us. It is manifesting an openness not just to this person's life, but to life in general. It is remembering that when someone did not listen to us we felt that we were not cared for by that person. It is believing that listening creates bonds of responsibility for another.

Listening, like other aspects of life that reveal who we are, suggests something that cuts through to an understanding of how we approach our own life as well as that of others. It reveals not only the ways in which we listen to ourselves and others, but it tells the most important truths about how we accept and return God's love for us. The interrelationship of the listening stance cannot be ignored. Invested efforts to listen to self, others and God are costly. We cannot do one and ignore the others. The world is all too familiar with the pseudo-prophet who claims to have heard messages from God while ignoring the clear life calls from self and others. We know equally well the fabrication of self-fulfillment that would dwell on self and reduce others to less than they are while denying God's love or even his existence.

THE LISTENER AS A PERSON OF PRAYER

God's word enters our lives in many ways. His call comes through events in the lives of nations and of individuals. His call comes in roaring thunder and in the gentle breeze. It touches us in spite of ourselves and because of ourselves. But only a call that is heard and listened to brings meaning and direction to life. Only a call that is shared brings the fullness of life.

Listening to God's call is directly related to our willingness and ability to listen to the call of a friend. Listening to God is the basis of our ability to listen to another. Unlike all others God's call is the only one which carries with it the promise of fulfillment as the call to friendship carries with it the possibility of discovering new life. Listening to God in prayer and listening to another in friendship are not separate realities. Like Samuel and Jeremiah we receive direction for our lives by listening to the message of God's call in searching for the meaning of our human experience.

Our attentiveness to the different ways we pray helps us understand the many ways in which we respond to one another in friendship. Our responsiveness to one another deepens our relationships with Father, Son and Spirit.

The listening person hears even while questioning who it is that speaks and what it is that the words mean:

> He (Samuel) got up and went to Eli and said, "Here I
> am, since you called me." Eli then understood that it
> was Yahweh who was calling the boy, and he said to
> Samuel, "Go and lie down, and if someone calls say,
> 'Speak, Yahweh, your servant is listening.'" . . .
> Yahweh then came and stood by, calling as he had
> done before, "Samuel! Samuel!" Samuel answered,
> "Speak, Yahweh, your servant is listening." Then
> Yahweh said to Samuel, "I am about to do such a
> thing in Israel as will make the ears of all who hear it
> ring."
>
> *I Samuel 3:9-11*

The listening person is given the responsibility of bringing
the word to others:

> Yahweh Sabaoth, the God of Israel, says this: For when
> I brought your ancestors out of the land of Egypt, I
> said nothing to them, gave them no orders, about
> holocaust and sacrifice. These were my orders: "Listen
> to my voice, then I will be your God and you shall be
> my people. Follow right to the end the way that I mark
> out for you and you will prosper." But they did not
> listen, they did not pay attention; they followed the dic-
> tates of their own evil hearts, refused to face me, and
> turned their backs on me.
>
> *Jeremiah 7: 21-24*

Stories like those of Samuel and Jeremiah and the
prophets of old will remain unrelated to my own life
unless I understand how God spoke and how they listened. If my image of the process is that of a heavenly
sound system with words being spoken directly and clearly, I may spend my life waiting for the same direction and
clarity. Certainly God can intervene in human lives in
this way. But the prophets and the messengers of old were
those who recognized and listened carefully to the signs of
the times. Yahweh was a Presence to them, a Companion

with whom they talked things over in much the same way we might do this with an absent friend or confidant. Those whose familiarity with the past and whose hopes for the future are a source of ongoing commitment to the present are the listeners. Their attentiveness to life, their courage and creativity in choosing to notice life at more than a superficial level, and their willingness to communicate to others that they see wins for them the respect of those searching for life's meaning and the rejection of those for whom the vision is too costly.

It is in the rich soil of the listening heart that all the qualities that prepare us to love self, others and God take root. It is in this same soil that the ability to make and keep commitments is nourished. It is in this rich soil that the profound mysteries in the life of each person unfold. It is out of this rich soil that prayer grows.

For most of us, our earliest ways of learning to pray were related to our reciting words we had committed to memory. We were able to say prayers that had many words we could scarcely pronounce and certainly did not understand. The example of Jesus validates this way of praying. We need to remember this in an age where we sometimes receive the impression that only "spontaneous prayer" is from the heart.

Throughout the life of Jesus we see him using the words of the Hebrew scriptures when he prays. He recites words that he has learned as a child. Nowhere is this more dramatically revealed than when Jesus is on the cross. The final words of Jesus are direct quotations from the Hebrew scriptures. Like Jesus, in crisis times, at times when we are not able to form words, when spontaneous conversation may not be possible for us, we need some words on which we can rely. Ask people who were in a tragic situation like an accident or a tornado what words they remember saying and, most often, if they prayed it was the words of some prayer that had been memorized.

Saying words is an important way of communicating with friends. So it is with our friend, God. But, just as there are other ways of sharing life with friends, so it is with our friend God. Friends discover that the closer they become the less need there is for continual conversation. One test of friendship is the comfort level of periods of silence. So it is with our friend God.

Saying words is one way of praying. Singing is "praying twice," some say. Work and play and all the other things we do as human beings have been given to God by those who learned the Morning Offering as school children. We say the Morning Offering knowing that it is a way of being in touch with God throughout our day.

But the way of being that is most at the heart of friend relationships—and one of the best ways of getting inside the meaning of our own lives—is that form of praying that is most difficult. It is the prayer that responds to God's words to Jeremiah and Samuel: "Listen to my voice." It is the prayer of listening.

How do I listen to God's voice? How do I become "the rich soil with a noble and generous heart?" One important beginning place is the understanding that the listening process is not different as it applies to self, others or God. It is not different as it applies to friend or enemy, young or old. The kind of listening of which Jesus speaks, a listening that hears, is a listening that goes far beyond sound waves and high scores on audio tests. It is a commitment to a way of life. It involves personal discipline, self-sacrifice and patience. It allows neither predetermined expectations nor hidden assumptions. It takes seriously good listening skills but goes far beyond them.

The rich soil of the listening heart has grown gradually to realize that, like the place at the edge of the path, the choice to be marginal to life, to remain distant from life is not a place of security but a place of self-destruction.

The rich soil of the listening heart has witnessed the surface life of the insensitive and the thoughtless. The person who lives in the whirlwind of endless activity and does not take time to deepen the sense not only of what is happening but what it means becomes a rocklike place that is unlikely to sustain life.

The rich soil of the listening heart has been prepared for life by recognizing that life places before us a never-ending series of choices. We cannot choose everything. We can refuse to make choices and become hopelessly indecisive and overwhelmed by the complicated network that engulfs us when we lack the courage to choose.

THE PRAYERFUL LISTENER AS FRIEND

Some of us have been blessed because we have had good teachers who taught us how to listen, when to listen and why to listen. They taught by their example more than by any words they spoke. We have been taught by parents who listened to us.

Rachel Carson, in her book *The Sense of Wonder,* says that if a child is to keep alive a sense of wonder, that child must have the loving companionship of at least one adult with whom to share that wonder. Together they can discover the joy and mystery of the world as they listen to its sounds and notice its beauty.

As a child some of my favorite times were days when I could go fishing or pheasant hunting with my father. My father loved the beauty of woods and lakes and fields. He noticed the birds in flight and the small animals that played along our path. He pointed out the mushrooms and the brightly colored flowers. He taught me to sit still

in the boat so that I could hear the fish jumping in nearby
waters. Always, there was a time when he said to me,
"Now close your eyes, be very still, and tell me every
sound you hear." When I failed to notice certain insect
sounds and some of the birdcalls, he'd ask me to listen
again until I had recognized more than just the obvious
ones.

I remember one afternoon when my father had gone
trout fishing. It was getting late and my mother sent a
neighbor to his favorite trout stream to see if he was all
right. That friend of my father loves to recount the story
of how he came upon my father, sitting under a tree
beside the peaceful stream, listening to the ducks and the
birds. His dry hip boots lay beside him. He had spent the
entire afternoon listening to the gentle movement of the
stream and the sounds of the birds and wild animals.

When we meet people for whom learning to listen is
not a personal goal we have a good opportunity to consider whether it is a goal for us. Noticing the qualities in
people who do not listen can help us see the value of being
a person who listens. Unless I have thought about the
qualities that I cherish in a listening friend or associate I
may, like the giver who never receives, be a speaker who
does not listen.

Jesus says to us, "Where your treasure is, there will
your heart be also" (Mt 6:21). He is reminding us of
something very basic. We do not sacrifice for and pay the
price of something that is not of value to us. Jesus is inviting us to ask ourselves the question: "Do I want to be a
good listener?" In so doing he links our ability to listen to
what we treasure.

Many Catholics tell me that one of the signs of
hopefulness they see in our church today is that the
church is becoming more of a listening presence. Men
and women, married and single, young and old, those

with special needs and those with gifts to give are being invited to participate in setting goals and establishing new channels of healing. The church, like each of its members, must be the rich soil that hears the word if it is to yield the harvest. It is in this rich soil that community grows.

A young man named Teddy is a 23-year-old cerebral palsy victim. He is in a wheelchair and cannot get into his parish church because it has no ramp. Teddy feels that no one has listened to him. He does not understand why churches are not subject to the same access laws as other public buildings. He wonders how to help people understand his life. He often says to me, "Think of how you would feel if you were the only one who could walk and everyone else in the world were in a wheelchair." He asks why people, in their own discomfort because of his physical disability, raise their voices with him. He smiles and says, "There is nothing wrong with my ears. Most people in wheelchairs are not deaf."

Teddy is a symbol of the difficulty we have in listening to those whose lives are, for a variety of reasons, different from our own. He is a reminder of our need to see beyond our differences in order to listen carefully and with sensitivity.

Listening encompasses a kind of all-inclusive attentiveness. It enriches the soil of the human heart. I remember visiting a friend I had not seen for several years. As I got off the bus, I noticed things about her neighborhood. As I climbed the stairs of her South Boston triple-decker, I was fascinated by the wooden railings and the elaborate woodwork. When she opened the door to her apartment, my attention was drawn to the colors she had selected for her draperies and carpet, to the pictures on her walls, to the many antique pieces she had collected. Her surroundings told me as much about her as any words we exchanged. Riding back to my hotel on the subway I realized that her home had told me as much about her as had her recounting of the years since our last visit. In a very real way, her home and neighborhood had spoken to me. I had listened to her surroundings as much as to her words.

The best example we have of a person whose life stance was that of a listener is Jesus. The quality of his listening is best revealed by the fruit that listening bore in the lives of those to whom he listened.

Jesus accepted hospitality from the hated tax collector, Zacchaeus. In doing so, he was well aware of the criticism of a crowd that wondered why he would stay at "a sinner's house." Jesus saw beneath the public image that imprisoned Zacchaeus. By listening to Zacchaeus he transformed him into a man who made plans to repair the harm that he had done to others (Lk 19: 1-10).

When the apostles complained about the crowds of parents who brought their children to Jesus, he lifted the children up, welcomed them and made of them an example of the faithful dwellers in the family of God. "Let the little children alone, and do not stop them coming to me; for it is to such as these that the kingdom of heaven belongs" (Mt 19:14). Jesus' desire to listen to the children was a reminder of the life that is to be found in seemingly unexpected places.

When Jesus spoke to the five-times-married Samaritan woman at Jacob's well his disciples manifested their surprise, "though none of them asked, 'What do you want from her?' or, 'Why are you talking to her?'" (Jn 4: 27). Listening to this woman made of her one of the first disciples of Jesus. By his listening to her this woman recognized that Jesus had brought her water that "will turn into a spring inside, welling up to eternal life" (Jn 4: 14).

Jesus listened to the impetuous Simon and the questioning Judas. He listened to the sons of Zebedee and the demands of their ambitious mother. Jesus listened to the rich young man who asked, "Good Master, what have I to do to inherit eternal life?" He told Jesus that he had kept the commandments from his birth. "And when Jesus heard this he said, 'There is still one thing you lack. Sell all that you own . . . then come, follow me' " (Lk 18: 19, 22-23). Those who came to Jesus with the expectation of being listened to were never disappointed. Because he had listened carefully to his own life, because he went apart to listen to his Father, Jesus possessed the inner quiet and resourceful security that are necessary for listening to others.

Jesus speaks to us about the meaning of life through the stories of his life. He speaks to us in the example of his relationships with others. Both the loving acceptance of his friends and the bitter hostility of his critics carry with them important messages for our lives. His never-ending need to balance quiet prayer time with the most intense and draining activity cannot be ignored by us. The example of the gentle and loving Jesus at Galilee cannot be separated from the forceful and confronting Jesus of Jerusalem. All three facets of his life came together in him in a way that we cannot forget if we wish to be Christians: his lifetime journey in self-discovery, his search for a way to give and receive friendship, and his place in the community he shared with the Father and the Spirit.

Like Jesus we will be transfigured if we listen carefully to the words on the mountain of the transfiguration:

> He (Peter) was still speaking when suddenly a bright cloud covered them with shadow, and from the cloud there came a voice which said, "This is my Son, the Beloved; he enjoys my favour. Listen to him."
>
> *Matthew 17: 5*

Like the disciples we may be afraid. We may doubt that

we can follow in Jesus' way and offer friendship to others as he did. Like the disciples, Jesus is there to reassure us as he listens to our faithful lives:

> When they heard this, the disciples fell on their faces, overcome with fear. But Jesus came up and touched them. "Stand up," he said, "do not be afraid."
>
> *Matthew 17: 6-7*

5 Becoming a separate self

> "The Son of Man" he said "is destined to suffer grievously, to be rejected by the elders . . . to be put to death. . . .
>
> "If anyone wants to be a follower of mine, let him renounce himself and take up his cross every day and follow me. For anyone who wants to save his life will lose it; but anyone who loses his life for my sake, that man will save it. What gain, then, is it for a man to have won the whole world and to have lost or ruined his very self?"
>
> *Luke 9: 22-25*

THERE IS an age-old tension between the ability to be who we are and the ability to be a friend. It is a tension between discovering who we are and sharing who we are. Some have called the relationship between the quest for self-identity and the search for self-giving in faithful friendship an impossible task. Others have ignored the presence of the tension.

Authentic relationships are rooted in our coming to terms with the basic aspects of the threefold relationship that is a part of Christian life: a relationship to self, others and God. The one thing that is clear is that to ignore any one of the three is to destroy the possibility of each of the others.

Without the sense of God's presence in our life we lack the most complete and richest source of the meaning of relationships. If we do not love and believe in ourselves we will not be able to offer the gift of self in friendship with the inner security which makes friendship possible. Unless we value the gift of another's presence in our life

73

we will not discover our own gift or find God. Becoming a separate self seems like a lonely and impossible task unless we understand the vital connections within this threefold relationship. Sometimes we approach the task from one dimension and sometimes from another, but we must not forget the others even when we are more attentive to one.

To look at the importance of our own selfhood it is helpful to reflect on the life of someone whose inner resources were strengthened in his search for this threefold relationship. The ever-present tensions of his life reveal the tensions that are a part of every life. The cost of his personal search for selfhood and friendship and faith is not different from ours.

On September 18, 1961, newspapers around the world proclaimed the sad news that one of the great leaders of all time had died in a plane crash near Ndola, Northern Rhodesia. Dag Hammarskjold, the Secretary-General to the United Nations, was respected by friends and enemies. Even his bitterest critics could question neither his integrity nor his dedication to world peace. The unprecedented eulogies given by the nations of the world were a dramatic reminder to our complex society that the presence of one good person touches an entire world.

What was not known at the time of his death and what was not revealed at the time of the tributes offered was the sustaining power and the source of strength for Hammarskjold's life. It was not until the publication of his *Markings* that the world learned that both the brilliant 'public servant and the sometimes timid private man were sustained by an inner person who drew his strength from the message of the Gospel and his sense of prayer from the writings of the great Christian mystics.

In a creed that Hammarskjold wrote for one of Edward R. Murrow's radio programs, he revealed the deepest message of his life:

> The explanation of how man should live a life of active social service in full harmony with himself as a member of the community of the spirit, I found in the writings of those great medieval mystics for whom "self-surrender" had been the way to self-realization, and who in "singleness of mind" and "inwardness" had found the strength to say Yes to every demand which the needs of their neighbors made them face, and to say Yes also to every fate life had in store for them. . . . Love—that much misused and misinterpreted word—for them meant simply an overflowing of the strength with which they felt themselves filled when living in true self-oblivion. And this love found natural expression in an unhesitant fulfillment of duty and an unreserved acceptance of life, whatever it brought to them personally of toil, suffering—or happiness.[1]

In this same creed, Hammarskjold spoke of the influence that the values of his parents had on his life. He was trained in the resourceful school of a family where deep personal convictions were the norm. He learned through the example of his father and mother that personal discipline and self-sacrifice are constitutive of life; that commitments made are kept and that the loneliness of leadership is not too high a personal price to pay for integrity. The presence of this family environment was reflected in the life of the four Hammarskjold brothers. It was generally known in public life in Sweden that "if there is a difficult task to be accomplished, give it to one of the Hammarskjolds and it will be done."

Hammarskjold was a mountain climber. His *Markings* were called by him "the trail marks" along his journey of life. They were his reminders for himself of the way that he had come, reflections he wanted to put in

[1] Hammarskjold, op. cit., Foreword.

writing to help him avoid past difficulties. He often applied his experience of climbing to his role in public life. He believed that the qualities of the climber are not different from those of any person who takes life seriously and lives with clearly established goals. The qualities of which he most often spoke were perseverance and patience, a good sense of the reality of a situation, creative and careful planning, a respect for the dangers involved and the conviction that the safest climber is one who never questions his ability to overcome the difficulties.

A part of the paradox of his life is not unlike our own. He was at once the outgoing public figure and the timid private man, the vocal and eloquent spokesman and the silent, reflective mystic, the tough, confrontive visionary and the sensitive, hurting pilgrim. His certainty on the journey rested in his belief that responsible decision-making gives life, just as remaining at the crossroads in indecision cuts off the possibility of life for self and others.

The world saw and recognized the admirable qualities of this prophet of peace and of world community. What he himself revealed to us later was the lonely and nearly despairing journey of his own human spirit. His was a spirit that was sustained by faith in God, by the presence of faithful friends, and by his adherence to his own hard-won personal integrity. His images of hunger and thirst along the way are ever-present themes in *Markings:*

> Hunger is my native place in the land of passions.
> Hunger for fellowship, hunger for righteousness—for a
> fellowship founded on righteousness, and a
> righteousness attained in fellowship.

> Only life can satisfy the demands of life. And this
> hunger of mine can be satisfied for the simple reason
> that the nature of life is such that I can realize my individuality by becoming a bridge for others, a stone in
> the temple of righteousness.

> Don't be afraid of yourself, live your individuality to
> the full—but for the good of others . . . .

> To become free and responsible. For this alone was
> man created, and he who fails to take the Way which
> could have been his shall be lost eternally.[2]

For Hammarskjold, not to become a person of service and
conviction, not to live a life that brings love and strength
to others is a life "lost eternally."

Other writers and public servants have spoken of the
same universal themes that are revealed in Hammarskjold's words and, to an even greater extent, in his life.
Thoreau reminded us of our need to listen carefully to the
drummer that we hear and to follow that drummer
however different or unfamiliar the rhythm may be.
Rainer Maria Rilke reminds us of the personal price paid
in every life that has meaning:

> Do not believe that he who seeks to comfort you lives
> untroubled among the simple and quiet words that
> sometimes do you good. His life has much difficulty
> and sadness. . . . Were it otherwise he would never
> have been able to find those words.[3]

Each of the prophets of the Hebrew scriptures speaks of
the challenges of listening to and interpreting the signs of
the times. Each speaks of the loneliness and lack of
understanding of most of their companions along the way.
Each saw and believed in a vision seen by no one else.
Each knew the feeling of being abandoned by others and
feared being abandoned by God.

The Israelites complained to Moses that they were
better off in Egypt claiming that he had brought them out
to the desert to die. The book of Exodus tells us of their
weariness and their angry discouragement through the
plagues:

[2] Hammarskjold, op. cit.

[3] Rainer Maria Rilke, *Letters to a Young Poet* (New York: W. W. Norton
& Co., Inc. 1963).

> And the whole company of the sons of Israel began to
> complain against Moses and Aaron in the wilderness
> and said to them, "Why did we not die at Yahweh's
> hand in the land of Egypt? . . . As it is, you have
> brought us to this wilderness to starve this whole com-
> pany to death."
>
> *Exodus 16: 2-3*

Jonah, sensing God's call to him to go to the people of
Nineveh and knowing the hardness and sinfulness of their
hearts, got on a ship heading in the opposite direction. He
knew the personal price of bringing an unpopular
challenge to a sinful people.

When the city of Jerusalem was besieged by the
Babylonians, Jeremiah manifested his belief in the
faithfulness of Yahweh and the future of this people by
purchasing a plot of land and proclaiming to disbelieving
skeptics, "People will buy fields and vineyards in this
land again" (Jer 32: 15).

Prophets of all ages see farther and with greater clarity than others. One of their gifted burdens is to live with
the loneliness that accompanies seeing what no one else
sees and having the courage to share the vision at
whatever personal cost.

Much has been written about the loneliness of the
leader. Contemporary writers have spoken of *The Lonely
Crowd, Loneliness and Love* and of *The Loneliness of the Long
Distance Runner.* Seminars and conferences are organized
around the topic of personal loneliness. It is a heritage we
share as human beings. It is a part of the price we offer in
exchange for discovering and cherishing who we are.

My experience and that of others leads me to a
distinction between the loneliness that is a part of the
uniqueness of every person's life journey and the
loneliness that results from circumstances about which we
can do something.

Each person's lifetime is a gradual unfolding of a single human personality. That unfolding is accompanied by the insecurity of the unknown and the fear of letting go of the known. Because each of us is different in history, temperament, convictions and experiences, life necessarily involves a sense of loneliness which can be the source of a rich creative tension as we discover our own growing edges and choose to reach beyond them. Rilke describes it this way:

> For if we think of this existence of the individual as a larger or smaller room, it appears evident that most people learn to know only a corner of their room, a place by the window, a strip of floor on which they walk up and down. Thus they have a certain security. And yet that dangerous insecurity is so much more human which drives the prisoners of Poe's stories to feel out the shapes of their terrible dungeons and not be strangers to the unspeakable terror of their abode.[4]

To seek to remove this kind of lonely experience would be to reduce the possibility of ever discovering the beauty and goodness that are ours, though hidden. But there is another kind of loneliness with which we can and must do battle. It is a loneliness that results from either an over-dependence on others or from giving in to a tendency to withdraw from others. It is the loneliness that is related as much to the expectation that someone else will fill the void within us as it is an inability or an unwillingness to share our life with others. This kind of loneliness may be typified by either of two extremes: the clutching, clinging person who resists becoming a separate self and the distancing, arrogant person who claims to need no one. It is only in and through relationships that we find the place in life that is somewhere between the two extremes that can destroy friendship: the expectation that someone else

[4] Rilke, op. cit.

can discover self for us and the futility expressed in the attitude that no one else's presence matters.

The only gift we have to give to another in friendship is the gift of self. We discover that gift as God calls our name and as we receive our name from others. Love is not fusion. Teilhard de Chardin says that love is the only force that unites human beings and brings them together in such a way as to bring out the best possibilities of each without depersonalizing either. To love in this way is possible only for the person who has been courageous enough to explore the unknown areas of Rilke's room while understanding that we cannot search in isolation.

No matter how close two human beings may be, there is yet great difference and distance between them. In fear and out of insecurity there is sometimes a subtle and subconscious effort to remove the differences and reduce the distance. We cannot love another unless we cherish the differences as a source of life and allow the distance to be a space of life where each reflects the goodness and beauty of the other. If we are frustrated by the differences and the distance that seem to separate us from others, we will become less than we are. If we see in those differences and in that distance the framework of a larger and richer life that we have not known, we recognize the invitation to become more than we are.

God who calls us to the richness of life and to the best of all its possibilities cannot free us from our loneliness. It is through that sense of aloneness that we will either reach out to him and to each other or we will seek the false security of isolation. In solitude we discover the hidden treasure of life, in isolation we destroy even the life that is there.

There is in each of us a public and a private person. God's call to life reminds us of the inner person that we come to know best in those self-reflective times when we are confronted with the uncharted and lonely way to selfhood. No one seeking the fullness of life can escape this loneliness. We find the fullness of life not in isolation but in relationship and we cannot enter into relationship with another unless we choose to explore the possibilities of our own existence. If we fail to go through the experience of realizing our separateness, we will not succeed in establishing bonds with another. The gift of friendship is an inside-out gift. When we give it, it goes out from the center of our existence and reaches into the center of another's life.

We cannot reach out to another unless we have some sense of who we are. We must know what it is that we offer in friendship. Unless we are our own person, it is difficult to know what gift we have to offer. Unless we have this sense of self, it is not possible for us to respect another. It is the uniqueness of each person's gift that is at once the source of the beauty and of the loneliness in friendship.

The only gift we have to offer may be given in confusion unless we have the courage to enter deeply into our own life to discover there the gift we offer. We may ask what another cannot give unless we allow another the personal space necessary for a self to grow and unfold. In relationship we risk giving more than we can and losing ourselves. Paradoxically, we can also lose ourselves by refusing to give what we know of who we are.

It is only by making this human journey that we can come to others and to God. Some Christians have tried to reverse this order of things. They set out to find God first because of their belief that this is the only journey that really matters. They did not listen carefully to the life of Jesus who is "the Word made flesh." They did not understand the words of John: "No one has ever seen God; but as long as we love one another God will live in

us'' (I Jn 4: 12). They failed to reflect on Jesus' words:
''What gain, then, is it for a man to have won the whole
world and to have lost or ruined his very self?'' (Lk 9: 25).
In these statements of John and Jesus rests the tension in
which relationships grow.

The journey of the human spirit of which we speak is
not an invitation to indulge in introspection. It is not a
cult of narcissism. It is not a lifelong commitment to inner
excavation. This inner journey is made not to lose
ourselves but to find ourselves. It is not withdrawal from
life but the firmest commitment to find life that can be
shared.

Jesus was his own person. Others could neither
manipulate him nor exert pressure that caused him to be
less than he was. For example, when Jesus responded to
the poor beggar at the Sheep Pool in Jerusalem, he was
criticized for helping the man on the sabbath. Jesus did
not allow the criticism of others to deter him from
responding to the needs of others. He was not paralyzed
by the continual attack from those who did not understand his seeming disregard for the law. He continued to
live according to the highest law he knew, the law of love.
The inner strength of Jesus sustained him:

> It was because he did things like this on the sabbath
> that the Jews began to persecute Jesus. His answer to
> them was: ''My father goes on working, and so do I.''
> But that only made the Jews even more intent on kill-
> ing him, because, not content with breaking the sab-
> bath, he spoke of God as his own Father, and so made
> himself God's equal.
>
> *John 5: 16-18*

Jesus knew well the price of listening carefully to his
Father's call, a call that led him on a journey that was to
cost him his life because of his faithfulness. Neither his
critics nor those who sought to harm him in the eyes of

others could divert Jesus from the lonely and demanding way of life to which he was committed. The rewards of that life are revealed in the kind of person Jesus was and in the example that he gives to us.

Jesus understood the cost of following the call because he had walked the same way in response to his Father. He lived in the never-ending demands of both his friends and enemies. His message to us of cross-carrying and self-denial is not poetic theory. He tells us that it is the only way we have of finding ourselves. It is the reassurance we have that coming to know and love ourselves and others was his task just as it is ours.

Just as God spoke to the prophets and leaders of his people, telling them of his presence, reassuring them of his love, so is God with us to bring courage and hope:

> Then Yahweh said: "So now brace yourself for action. Stand up and tell them all I command you. Do not be dismayed at their presence. . . . I, for my part, today will make you into a fortified city, a pillar of iron, and a wall of bronze to confront all this land. . . . They will fight against you but shall not overcome you, for I am with you to deliver you—it is Yahweh who speaks."
>
> *Jeremiah 1: 17-19*

It is Yahweh who speaks to us, offering to make us into pillars of iron and walls of bronze who have the courage to search for the vision of our lives and for the commitment to follow the vision once it is seen by us.

Jesus told his closest friends of the troubled times they would face. He spoke to them about the cost of discipleship. He reminded them of their need for deep personal convictions that are unshakeable in the face of misunderstanding and hostility. He promised to be with them, showing them the way of life:

> Listen, the time will come . . .
> when you will be scattered, each going his own way
> and leaving me alone.

And yet I am not alone,
because the Father is with me.
I have told you all this
so that you may find peace in me.
In the world you will have trouble,
but be brave:
I have conquered the world.

John 16: 32-33

Those of us who have chosen to bear the name Christian
are asked to walk the way that Jesus walked. Like Jesus,
we have the reassuring and strength-giving love of God
with us always. We walk in the presence of the Spirit of
Jesus and are the recipients of the Spirit's gifts.

Like the prophets of old, like Jesus, like the saints we
emulate and like contemporaries who, by their example,
give us courage and hope, we are called to catch hold of
our souls in the lonely places where convictions become
our own. Like them we then reach out to those with whom
we journey. Like them we learn and are inspired by the
example of those who would not exchange the gains of the
world at the price of the loss of self.

Dag Hammarskjold wrote: "As I continued along
the Way, I learned, step by step, word by word, that
behind every saying in the Gospels stands *one* man and *one*
man's experience." As we continue along the way we,
too, learn that a person stands behind the word of the
Gospel. That person is Jesus, our way. He calls us to
stand behind the word of the Gospel with our lives. He
calls us to walk in friendship, knowing that we can be a
friend to another person only if we have the courage to be
ourselves.

6 The seasons of friendship

> There is a season for everything,
> a time for every occupation under
>   heaven:
> a time for giving birth, a time for
>   dying;
> a time for planting, a time for
>   uprooting what has been planted. . . .
> A time for tears, a time for laughter;
> a time for mourning, a time for
>   dancing. . . .
> a time for keeping silent, a time for
>   speaking. . . .
> A time for loving. . . .
>
> *Ecclesiastes 3: 1-2, 4, 7*

THE WRITER of the book of Ecclesiastes, like writers of our own time, reminds us that the seasons of the year reflect the variations that are a part of the fabric of every life. Theologians speak of the ways in which the sacraments are intimately linked with the seasons of human life: baptism and birth, confirmation and coming of age, marriage or holy orders and adult life, the sacrament of the sick and the golden years. The sacraments reflect initiation into life and the ongoing growth that is a part of life.

Sociologists and behavioral scientists give attention, as did Sam Levinson, to *The Seasons of a Man's Life.* Gail Sheehy's popularized version of this research, *Passages,* has been widely read. The attractiveness of these works to the reading public is indicative of the universal appeal that is present in relating the search for human meaning

85

to the ways in which the seasons of the earth provide a helpful framework for such personal reflection. It is that same framework which relates the seasons of life to the seasons of friendship.

Certainly the writing of others helps clarify and set in perspective the meaning of the seasons, but our best teacher remains the challenge of human experience—our own and that of others. My insight into the seasons of human life was immeasurably enriched by an old man named Bowman. The seasons of life and of friendship were reflected in his eyes, in the stories he told me, in the old violin and typewriter he carried, but, most of all, in his manner.

I had been in a small town in northern Minnesota giving a talk. I left the airport with a few other passengers. I noticed that one of the passengers, a kindly looking old man, was carrying a violin case and a very old portable typewriter.

When I reached my assigned place on the plane, I discovered that I was sitting next to that man. He was silent as we took off. For a long time he looked out the window. I wanted to respect his silence—believing that he might not want to talk. A few minutes later, I realized that he was looking at me out of the corner of his eye. I turned to him, smiled, and said, "Hello. How far are you flying today?" He told me that he was on his way to South Carolina to live with a daughter. Then he added, "It's not easy to leave. I have so many friends here. But, there will be friends there, too. You always find friends if you look for them."

He explained to me that he had been a custodian at the high school in the town that we were leaving. He told of how the past year's graduating class had given him an award which read "To Our Friend Bowman." He said, "When I walked down the streets of that town everyone who lived there knew me. I have been at the school for 35 years. I loved it there. Young people spoke to me and laughed at my stories. They knew I was their friend. They could always count on Bowman. Now, I am too old to work anymore and I must leave. My arthritis is bad. Look at my fingers.''

A twinkle came into his eyes when he said, ''I play the violin. I've played my violin so that lots of people could dance and have good times. I have my violin with me. I'd be lonely without it. Playing the violin and carving were the ways I made other people happy. I have carved furniture for the homes of fine folk and I have carved toys for the kids that play in the street. I've brought a lot of happiness into the lives of others in that small town. I'll find friends in South Carolina even though I'm not able to carve or play like I used to. My life is like the seasons. Like each season it brings me new blessings. My daughter will be good to me. She always loved her dad. She was proud of my fiddling and my carving. I thought she'd want this old typewriter. She used to play with it when she was a little girl.''

Bowman told me stories of friends—of people who had shown love to him. As I listened to him, he paused and said, ''But you aren't interested in all this talk from an old man. Thank you for listening to me. It was hard to leave my friends and get on this plane. You have made this part of the trip easier. I hope I find my plane in Minneapolis. I have never been in that airport and I guess you could get lost there.'' I told him that I knew the airport well and would walk with him to his gate and check his next connection with him.

I waited until his plane left. As he was ready to board the plane, he kissed me on the cheek and said, ''Thanks for listening to me and for being my friend. Old Bowman will remember to pray for you.''

That gentle man, that man whose eyes reflected his inner happiness as he told stories of his "fiddling and carving days," was a reminder to me of the important ways we bring life to one another. Somehow I envied the young people in whose school he had worked, young people who called old Bowman their friend. If they listened to him they had gained some wisdom about the seasons of his life and of their own. If they listened to Bowman, they had learned about the seasons of friendship.

Like the seasons in the life of Bowman and the seasons of which he spoke, there is a goodness and beauty in each of nature's seasons. Each season has its own unique role to play in the process of life and growth. Those seasons with which we associate the most recognizable periods of growth stand in contrast to those during which life seems to be dormant. Without the death and decay which is characteristic of other seasons, the earth would not be replenished and prepared for the bursting forth of new life in spring.

When we take time to observe the changes in the earth, when we look for the parallels between all life and our own lives, we discover that the work of the creator manifests the wisdom of life. Noticing the goodness and beauty in the world around us gives us a sense of conviction about the presence of that same goodness and beauty in the seasons of our own lives—seasons whose richest meaning is reflected in friendship.

The earth cannot resist growth and change. The earth cannot interfere with the coming of its own seasons. The seasons recur as a part of a plan that is larger than the earth. They are related to a wisdom that carries with it a time-tested plan. The ancients noticed the recurrence of the seasons. What they failed to notice and to understand was that human life has one dramatic difference. The seasons of human life do not recur in the inevitable and mathematical manner predicted by nature's clocks. The seasons of human life do not just happen, they are related to the decisions we make or fail to make. For us the seasons of life are related to decisions that others make or fail to make. Unlike the earth, we determine the seasons of our lives. We determine them by listening carefully to God's ever-present call to life and by responding to that call as it unfolds for us. It is in embracing the seasons of our lives because of God's call and our response to that loving call that the seasons of human life can bring with them the same possibility for life that we find in the seasons of the earth. We embrace the seasons of life only as we embrace the meaning of the two great commandments. We cannot choose our seasons in isolation.

The changing of the seasons is like the turning-point times in human life. Like the seasons of the earth that seem to challenge and threaten life, the crisis times of human life are rich sources of ever-present and dangerous opportunities for new life. Like the seasons of the earth, the uncertainty of changing times opens us to renewed life only through courageous risks for life. Like the result of the falling and decay of leaves that is revealed only in the richness of soil that gives new life in spring, so the resurrection time of human life becomes apparent only after we have walked through the darkness of an ending to a new beginning. Like plants growing up through dead leaves in order to turn the faces of the new leaves to the sun, so the human conversion experience turns us again and again to God's love and to our need for each other's friendship.

Just as the seasons of the earth come and go, year after year, so do the opportunities for the seasons of human life. Like the seasons of the earth, the seasons of our lives are never complete. We are invited to make the journey through the seasons of our lives and the journey of human friendship not once but repeatedly. With each turning-point time, with each journey through another season of life, with each journey in friendship, we learn something more about ourselves, we become better companions to others and we realize more fully God's everpresent love and strength.

Each season through which we journey involves a letting go of what is present and an openness to what lies ahead. We are like Abraham as he stands at the threshold of a new season of his life.

> Yahweh said to Abram, "Leave your country, your family and your father's house, for the land I will show you. I will make you a great nation; I will bless you and make your name famous so that it will be used as a blessing."
>
> *Genesis 12:1, 2*

Abraham's name is blessed among us as one who had the courage to trust this new season of his life because he had listened carefully to his life. He knew that he was not making the journey alone because he trusted that God's love would be manifested all along the way. Like Abraham, we are blessed because God gives us the gift of many seasons each of which holds an important key to new and renewed life. Like Abraham, we are blessed by God as we walk into the recurring seasons of friendship, seasons whose gifts and struggles we can either choose or reject. When we take time to consider the most obvious characteristics of each season, the qualities of the seasons of friendship become more apparent to us.

SPRING: THE NEWNESS OF FRIENDSHIP

In springtime, the days grow longer as tender new life emerges. There is an excitement about spring. When we see the new life all around us, we feel more alive. The fresh spring greens bring with them a heightened awareness of the goodness and beauty of life. The contrast of spring with the season of winter which has just passed arouses in us a fascination with the mystery of life. It is a time of vulnerability for the new life that emerges everywhere. There is a preoccupation with life. Little attention is given to the dormant and the dying.

So it is with the springtime of friendship. There is an excitement about the ease with which new friends share and discover together. Self-revelation is not a challenge when we give the gift of that which we already know. When relationships are new, the discovery process is wondrous and open. The gratitude for the new gift contributes to a kind of growth in which intimacy can deepen. The rewarding awareness of life received is the center of attentiveness rather than the haunting fear of personal vulnerability. New friendships seem easier to sustain because there has been no time of testing, no history of failure, no past memory of coldness or conflict. It is a time to notice the life that is there and growing. This season is, therefore, a time of hope. The springtime of friendship is described in the Song of Songs:

> Come then, my love,
> my lovely one, come.
> For see, winter is past,
> the rains are over and gone.
> The flowers appear on the earth.
> The season of glad songs has come.
> *Song of Songs 2:10-12*

The beauty of spring and the spontaneity of its growth provide a challenge to every friendship to keep some of spring alive in each season that will follow.

SUMMER: THE GROWTH OF FRIENDSHIP

Summer is a time of sunshine days. The new and tender life that began earlier is warmed and sustained. In summer, fragile life grows strong. The spring green is transformed into the deeper green that is responsible for the food-making process. Summer days create an atmosphere of playfulness and relaxation in people who have waited through the cold of winter and the increasing warmth of spring. The growth of summertime replaces the dramatic bursting forth of spring with the persistent, maturing life of summer.

The summertime of friendship exchanges the excitement of having found a new friend for the quiet awareness that this season is less fragile. It is a season of inner security and of more steady and surer communication. Like the summer after the spring planting time, it is a time of "let it be" and "let it grow." There is a sense of coming to feel at home with a friend no longer "new."

The best of summer is that life which remembers the beginnings of spring and grows so well that it is preparing, even subconsciously, for the transition to fall and winter. The summer of friendship is a time of thankfulness, a time of gratitude for God's gifts and those of my friend.

> I thank my God whenever I think of you; and every time I pray for you, I pray with joy, remembering how you have helped me to spread the Good News from the day you first heard it right up to the present. I am quite certain that the One who began this good work will see that it is finished. . . . You have a permanent place in my heart. . . .
>
> *Philippians 1:3,6,7*

Singers tell us of "The Good Old Summertime" and of "Summer, when the livin' is easy." Their songs are a reminder to love these days well and to love so well during these days that we carry their goodness into the seasons that follow.

FALL: THE LONELINESS OF FRIENDSHIP

Of all the seasons, fall carries with it the greatest sense of melancholy, a longing for what has been and a reluctance to enter into that which is ahead. The transition from summer to fall begins in a nearly imperceptible way, passes into the time of glorious color and then fades into darker hues. It is a season that takes us from the warm dependability of summer to the unpredictability of fall temperatures. Robert Frost, in his poem "Reluctance," captures the mood of the season when he speaks of the dead leaves on the ground and of those that "the oak is still keeping." He tells us of the loneliness of the last aster and of the inner spirit: "The heart is still aching to seek, but the feet question 'Whither?' "

In this season of friendship we come to terms with our own loneliness, a part of life that no friend or lover can take away from us. It is a time when, having shared all that we know of ourselves with a friend, we are confronted with the ongoing journey in self-discovery, a journey that no one can make for us. It is in coming to terms with our own inner space that we are free enough to give space to another. It is in listening carefully to this turning time of the year that we are strengthened to hear the messages from this lonely inner place and to walk on with a friend who must do the same. We need this inner solitude in order to love well. In solitude and self-reflection times we become more present to ourselves and have more to share with another. Rilke says, "Love consists in this that two solitudes love and protect each other."

It is in this season of the year when life is preparing for the dying time that we are reminded of the necessity of letting go of some life that we have known in order to discover life that is not yet ours.

Seldom do two friends grow in the same way and at the same rate. There is an insecurity in growing to a place new to me and yet unknown to my friend. To walk in love and hope, we need the reassurance that accompanies the belief that we are never walking through any season alone. Jesus who knows well the seasons of the human journey is there as friend and companion to reassure us:

> Do not let your hearts be troubled,
> Trust in God still, and trust in me.
> There are many rooms in my Father's house;
> if there were not, I should have told you.
> I am now going to prepare a place for you. . . .
> You know the way to the place where I am going.
>
> *John 14: 1,2,4*

When Jesus tells us that we "know the way," it is because he believes in the seasons of companionship and trusts our faithful response to his Father's call to life. Jesus trusts our ability to find life in every season.

WINTER: THE FAITHFULNESS OF FRIENDSHIP

Winter is a time of quiet life. It is a season devoid of the obvious growth of spring and summer. It is a season that lacks the vibrancy of the color time of fall. The winter sun warms, but not with the same rays that find us in the other seasons. There is a stillness about winter. Unlike the persistent sound of falling rain, even the snow that falls comes silently. The gardens and places of growing plants and trees are covered by a blanket, whether of snow or of pine needles, that gives an urgency to our long-ing for spring. Our belief that this, too, is a time of life depends more on our memory of the life we have seen than on that which is present around us now. We know that this season is not less important than the others. We know that the cycle of life is completed during this time when plants and trees rely on food that was stored in summer. Periods of dormancy are not less life-giving than times of activity. Just as winter is a place of life so times of self-reflection and solitude nourish and sustain the human spirit. Quiet times gives direction to our lives.

Friends who have grown to a place of comfortable and loving silence have an insight into the season of winter. It is the season of faithfulness to commitments. The need for the excitement of spring, the steady and perceptible growing time of summer, and the rich color of fall are replaced by a reassuring conviction that this is a time to celebrate the life that has grown and been nourished. It is a time to rely on the decisions and the willingness to share life that have been a part of every other season. Just as the food that sustains the tree was prepared and stored during the other seasons, so the investment made in the other seasons of friendship now comes to fruition. It is a time of reflective quiet when friends experience the wisdom and the rewards of having invested well in each of the other seasons.

> A faithful friend is a sure shelter,
> whoever finds one has found a rare treasure.
> A faithful friend is something beyond price,
> and there is no measuring his worth.
> A faithful friend is the elixir of life.
>   *Ecclesiasticus 6: 14-16*

Each of the seasons gives a special quality to a friendship. The romantic notions of love and friendship which surround us and which can contribute to the destruction of friendship may not sustain us through the costly variations of the seasons. The easy attraction patterns and the unrealistic expectations too often associated with what it means to be a friend or to have a friend will not lead us to the "sure shelter" and the "rare treasure" described in Ecclesiasticus. Every season is a season of faithfulness because each invites a commitment asked by no other season. It is because we have been faithful to each season of friendship that we recognize what faithfulness means when we experience the life-sustaining quiet of the winter season.

THE SEASONS OF LIFE AND OF FRIENDSHIP: A STUDY IN CONTRASTS

The journey through the seasons of friendship is a study in contrasts. With each repeated journey through each season of every friendship we discover some new meaning. We are surprised and delighted when we gain some new insight that would have us say, "This is it! This is what friendship is all about." Then, just as quickly, life moves on and we find ourselves asking again the questions we have asked before. We also ask questions that we have not thought about before. And we begin again to study the contrasts and shapes out of which will come another insight, another way to say, "This is what friendship is."

All of life is a study in contrasts. Most of life is lived somewhere in between extremes that we learn to recognize. We fear, alternately, the unknown and the known. We walk through trying periods of darkness and uncertainty into a clarifying light that is too much for us. When the path to a life-giving future is too frightening for us, we retreat to the past as if to stay there forever. When the cost of friendship and community asks its inevitable price, we look longingly toward the isolation of the desert claiming that it is more of God.

Each of us has lived through the seasons of many years and many friendships. We have been surrounded by the obvious beauty of those seasons and have rejoiced in the goodness of each. We have seen the seeming destructiveness of some of the seasons and we have been afraid. Perhaps we have given way to a kind of boredom that takes less notice of the beauty. Perhaps we have seen all too clearly the personal implications of the seasons when death is more apparent than life.

If we fail to notice the contrasts that point out where life is, we will not discover it. Life makes its own demands. We may grow weary or afraid and decide that the cost is too great. But we can make choices that nature cannot make. We can choose or reject the challenge of the seasons of our lives.

The earth does not choose its seasons. They simply recur. In one sense this lets the earth free to enter into each season unhindered and to experience the fullness and goodness of each. Unlike the earth, we are called to enter into the seasons of life and of friendship by the personal choices we make. Our experience tells us that it is only through this journey that life is to be found. We choose each season of life and of friendship risking the life that we have for the life that we believe is possible. If we refuse this choice or choose only halfheartedly we will miss not only the hidden goodness of each season but we will never discover the hidden person that is revealed only in friendship.

7 Recognizing the pitfalls to friendship

> When I was a child, I used to talk like a child, and think like a child, and argue like a child, but now I am a man, all childish ways are put behind me. Now we are seeing a dim reflection in a mirror; but then we shall be seeing face to face. The knowledge that I have now is imperfect; but then I shall know as fully as I am known.
>
> In short, there are three things that last: faith, hope and love; and the greatest of these is love.
>
> *I Corinthians 13:11-13*

THE PROBLEM with the destructive elements in friendship is that we discover them so slowly that we may have destroyed the possibility of being friends before we recognize the difficulty. The school of friendship has no advanced learners. There are no "born geniuses." There is only the way of the prodding and persistent achiever whose commitment to and recognition of the importance of the goal is not doubted. There is only the way of the faithful Christian who has heard and understood the meaning of the two great commandments as one commandment, a commandment to love self, others and God.

Discovering the subtle and subconscious facets of our ways of relating to others is a costly personal project. It requires gentle patience with ourselves and an ability to forgive ourselves for not having done what we did not know how to do at any given time. The oft-repeated phrase "if only I had known then what I know now" loses its self-destructive quality when we use "what we know now" as a direction-finder for the future rather than as a regret-perpetuator of the past.

99

There is no easy school for friendship. There are no short courses on caring. The invitation from God to become a friend, even to one person, is at the heart of the Gospel call to love. It is an invitation that is not for the fainthearted. In this invitation is contained the only way to full human life.

Children sometimes have a way of verbalizing the most profound philosophy for life. Their simple manner of expression, devoid of a distracting eloquence, can frame life's experience in unforgettable ways.

A friend of mine was putting her three-year-old son, Eric, to bed. Because he did not want to go to bed, he did everything he could to prolong the conversation with his father and mother. Recognizing a tactic Eric had often used before his mother said to him, "It is time for you to go to sleep now. Your father and I are going to put out the light after we kiss you goodnight." He responded with the protest, "But I'm afraid in the dark." His mother, whose patience was being tried, said, "There is nothing to be afraid of. God is here with you." Eric looked up at his father and mother and said, "I know that God is here, but I want someone in here with skin on."

A theologian could take Eric's words and form them into a very down-to-earth explanation of the incarnation, the Word made flesh. God knew that we needed someone with "skin on" to walk with us and so he gave us his son, Jesus.

A behavioral scientist or a process philosopher might recognize in Eric's words the story of the ongoing growth of the human person. From this perspective we could say that the task of life is "to get our skins on" and to learn to live in the human condition with a skin that is often uncomfortable and always a challenge. Coming to understand, accept and cherish our human skins is one way to describe each person's Christian pilgrimage. Growing in the ability to accept and cherish the human skins of others is what we call friendship and community.

Few influences around us help us understand and accept ourselves and others. Little of what we hear and see in the media gives us insight into what it means to be a good friend to anyone. Songs tell us that these are not easy times for lovers and friends because of the "I want to be free" and "I gotta be me" priorities that people bring to relationships. What the songs do not tell us is what it means to be free and how we discover who we are so that we can be who we are. All too often their words fluctuate between the cult of self-indulgence which destroys personal moral fiber and the cold, dehumanizing sterility of isolation. When we hear the "don't think, feel" approach we are confused by the undue emphasis on feelings as though they are all there is to life. Yet we have nearly been destroyed by an approach that made feelings suspect and therefore to be denied or repressed.

Conflict avoidance patterns are one of the major destructive elements in friendship. From the starry-eyed influence of "love means you never have to say you are sorry" to the "tell it like it is" extremes, we look for a life-giving way. But the people who sing the songs and who write the television scripts do not provide helpful ways to discover the truth about the meaning of friendship and love.

The cult of sex would have us believe that the highest good to be sought in relationships is to be found in sexual compatibility. The experience of all too many lost relationships alerts us to the tragedy of an inverted order when people are lovers first, then marry or live together without asking if they were friends.

People with deficient self-images enter into relationships with the expectation that "half will be made whole" by someone else. This harmful half-truth is sometimes not recognized for what it is because the affirmation of friends does help us become more than we might have been without their love.

It is one thing to acknowledge that someone is important to me; it is quite another to believe and thus enslave ourselves and another with the too often heard expression "I cannot live without you." To be loved is freeing, never enslaving. To love is to touch another's life, not to clutch at it in a dependent manner. Possessiveness signals some inner insecurity that interferes with giving and receiving in faithful friendship. Friendship involves sharing life, not possessing it.

The impact on us of cultural and so-called religious influences may be so subtle as to be nearly imperceptible. We learn to love only by continuing to try to love. Our imperfect responses and our sinfulness can obscure the meaning of friendship. Unless we are to repeat past errors and continue to hurt ourselves and others, it is important for us to find some touchstones against which to test the truth of our experience. We need to find some place more reliable than current thought and lifestyles. We need something more substantial than dealing with love as if it were nothing more than a mutual set of attraction patterns. We search for that which will help transform our imperfect ways of loving into friendship that is mutually life-giving. To do this we must put aside the questions that may temporarily obscure the real questions. We need something more substantial than the romantic notion that love is "soft as an easy chair." We need courage and common sense to be faithful to friendship.

Although the following incident happened several years ago, speaking of it now heightens the memories. Jim and Sandy had been giving some consideration to marriage. The "problem," as they described it, was that Sandy considered herself an agnostic. Their concern was that

Jim's parents would object strongly to a wedding involving even a Christian of another tradition and would never be open to his marrying someone with no professed religious beliefs. After a series of appointments during which we discussed the basic tenets of the Catholic faith and of Christianity, Sandy said that she was beginning to realize that she was not an agnostic. She said she had never had an opportunity to learn what faith in God meant and what it asked. She said that she felt open to pursuing the study of Christianity that we had begun.

With the question of religion now a lesser one, I asked Jim and Sandy if there were anything else that they wanted from me. Knowing that I had been involved in marriage preparation at the parish, they asked for some time in which to look into other aspects of their friendship. Once the religious question was no longer paramount in their minds, they had some sense of deeper and more basic questions. I had an uneasiness about their inability to speak of their friendship in any other way than to say that they shared a "common set of ideals."

In preparation for our next meeting I asked each of them to take a piece of paper and write down all the things they shared and liked to share. On the back side of the paper I asked them to write the things they did not or would not share. I asked them then to come separately to see me. The long list of things they did not share was much the same for both of them. Part of it read something like this:

—We do not like each other's friends, and so we don't cross social circles.

—We like different kinds of music. (He liked hard rock; she preferred classical music and each resisted going with the other for an evening of music.)

—We have different ways of budgeting and planning how to spend money. (She liked to save her money and lived very frugally. He believed that money should be spent as soon as possible.)

—We have different recreational interests. (He liked the out-of-doors and frequently enjoyed backpacking. She liked no outdoor activity.)

—We have different tastes in food. (He was very serious about health requirements and natural foods. She liked beer and pizza.)

Not surprisingly, the side of the paper revealing what they shared was nearly blank. Both said that they believed they liked each other and shared the same values.

By this time, the implications of these lists were no longer hidden from them. Each admitted that the predictions for the future of their friendship were not good. Each realized that there was very little related to the staying-power of friendship in their care for one another. Each gave as a final reason for pursuing the friendship a fear that "I might not meet someone else and then what will I do?" Unlike many people in similar circumstances, Jim and Sandy had the courage and the good sense to end the relationship. All too often, given the same evidence, this is the point at which some people choose marriage.

Jim and Sandy were not insensitive or unintelligent. They were the near-victims of a cultural pressure which couples people before they develop a sense of selectivity in determining where the sustaining power of friendship is and where it is not. They had given little serious thought to the qualities out of which good friendships are fashioned.

Every friendship is a challenge to our inner darkness and selfishness. When we come to terms with this challenge in one friendship it gives us more freedom and creativity in another. When we understand this, we realize that no friendship is ever really lost if we enter into it in the best way we know at the time. The end of every friendship, just as truly as the beginning of each, is an opportunity for renewed life if we choose to make it so.

But it is possible to learn nothing from failed friendship. When we fail to learn we bring emptiness and not fullness to the possibility of another friendship. Unless we have the wisdom and courage to look at what failed as well as to rejoice in what succeeded, much of our dearly bought experience may be lost to ourselves and to others.

When we are too close to a relationship some ways to find distance and space are important. The eyes of others may see what we fail to see. Our inability to see the troublesome patterns involved in a relationship may cause repetition of these same patterns in a new relationship. We must come to some turning point that reveals to us now what we failed to see at an earlier time. We need faithful friends who will call us to life by telling us what they see, even when we resist what they tell us because we see it differently. Often when we ask friends later what they saw, they can tell us with accuracy what we failed to see. But we are not helped by those who would impose their insights on us.

Meeting a friend, having a friend, being a friend—there are few hours of our lives that are not related to one of these. We do few things that do not touch on friendship and our faithfulness to it. Like so many other things that are carefully woven into the fabric of our existence, we may be too close to notice or observe the patterns. The too familiar hues and contrasts may fail to claim our attention even when they signal to us some change or impending danger. Like the watchful servant, we must notice and interpret the signs that we read. If we are to put aside a childhood vision, if we are to come to terms with an imperfect manner of loving, then, like Jim and Sandy, we sometimes need to take an inventory of our way of being a friend. We cannot afford to be blind to the pitfalls. Neither can we continue to live with the dim reflection of friendship. God's call to life and our call to be a better friend to each friend, are one.

T. S. Eliot in his poem "Ash Wednesday" says, "Suffer us not to mock ourselves with falsehood. Teach us to care and not to care." This is a strong invitation from Eliot to come to understand the realities of caring so that we will not be caught in the fabrications.

If we are to learn "to care and not to care" we can look to only one reference place. We look to a God whose caring and not caring reflect at once the tough and tender faces of his love for us. We look to a God who reveals to each of us all of life's best possibilities only through our repeated and sometimes failing efforts to care and not to care for ourselves and others. We look to a God in "human skin" who shared our journey in friendship. In sharing with us the example of his way of being a friend and of having friends, Jesus takes us far beyond the illusions of friendship. He calls his friends to look at the example of his life.

> On the following day as John stood there again with two of his disciples, Jesus passed, and John stared hard at him and said, "Look, there is the lamb of God." Hearing this, the two disciples followed Jesus. Jesus turned round, saw them following and said, "What do you want?" They answered, "Rabbi,"—which means Teacher—"where do you live?" "Come and see," he replied.
>
> *John 1:35-39*

Jesus says to each of us, "Come and see." He invites us to see beyond the fads and oversimplified systems that would have us believe that learning to be a friend is as simple as one weekend workshop. He invites us to be open to the rich variety of human experiences, each of which is some small part of the fabric of friendship. He challenges us to be selective as we evaluate opportunities for learning how to be a friend and understanding that we cannot really be a friend if our primary concern is taking care of number one.

At a recent weekend retreat I asked the participants to make a list of five factors in our culture that they considered to be the most destructive to friendships. After each person had listed "Five Pitfalls to Friendship" we shared our ideas. The following represents those repeated most often.

THE MARRIAGE-ORIENTED SOCIETY IN WHICH WE LIVE

Most of our culture continues to reflect the attitude that everyone ought to be married. This is seen in the very early ways that we "couple" young children. Society's expectation that everyone will or ought to marry encourages the dating patterns that too often destroy or dwarf the meaning of friendship.

Our preoccupation with marriage as the fullest and only recognized form of friendship has deprived us of the richness that can be found in deep friendships with persons either of the same or of the opposite sex. All too often a man or a woman who is planning to be married terminates all other relationships in order to spend all of the time with that one person. This same preoccupation with marriage often leads those who have lost a partner through death or divorce into another marriage long before their grieving is sufficiently complete to bring them to the place of emotional stability necessary for entering into a new relationship.

Some women measure their attractiveness by how they attract men. This attitude is just as destructive of men as it is of women. The dominant marrying mood in our society places both people in any relationship in a position of disadvantage.

The compulsion to marry (or to couple and live as if married) has reversed the good order in relationships which once gave people time to explore and cherish the possibilities of friendship before they chose to marry and/or become lovers. Many disillusioned lovers wish they had understood that the staying power in friendships involves much more than sexual compatibility. Many lovers lack the inner resources they need to discover whether or not they share enough of life's experience to be good friends.

Romantic notions of loving

As long as we continue to equate love with feelings of attraction and continue to believe that love and conflict are incompatible, we will live with the superficial notions of love that afflict people who enter into relationships. No one would argue against the importance of feelings of attraction, but we destroy love if we believe that they represent all of loving.

Our feelings give us some important leads, but they do not take us far enough along the way. Friendship involves much more than how we feel, however vital it is that we recognize how we feel. Friendship is related to what we believe, what we know, what we choose, what we value, and what we pursue even when it asks suffering of us.

Our feelings sometimes rise up in us out of undetermined and unrecognized sources. We feel different ways on different days even about people and convictions that we value. Romantic love places undue emphasis on the role of feelings in friendship. Like sexual compatibility in marriage, our tender feelings are but one component of faithful friendship. We destroy friendship when we make feelings either more or less important than they are. Dostoevsky describes this well when, in *The Brothers Karamazov,* he says that love in dreams is easy, that romantic notions of loving are comfortable and warming, but "real love is a harsh and dreadful reality." Romantic notions of love are part of the "imperfect knowledge of love" of which St. Paul speaks.

REFUSAL TO ACCEPT THE ROLE OF CONFLICT IN FRIENDSHIP

The harm of the myth that "love means you never have to say you are sorry" is not that it introduced a new idea. The harm is that it reinforced already existing fears in the insecure, and strengthened the false belief that anger and love are not compatible. Further, it failed to acknowledge the destructiveness of avoiding conflicts in relationships.

The writer of the book *Creative Aggression* suggests that marriage vows should be changed from "Love, honor and obey" to "Love, fight and grow." While there is an element of wisdom in this suggestion, it presupposes that people know how to "fight" constructively. It overlooks the destructiveness of those who "fight" and destroy or devastate rather than entering into conflict in such a way as to call another to life.

Our ways of dealing with anger and frustration are the culprits in all of this. To the extent that we have been programmed to look upon anger as an unacceptable or an unchristian response, to that extent we will be unable or unwilling to deal with conflict. We will not recognize conflict as a call to abandon the imperfect way of love so that we may learn better ways of loving. We are not called to ways of loving that mask or deny feelings that can only destroy friendship when they are ignored. We are called to the difficult personal task of being in touch with our

feelings and of taking personal responsibility for expressing them. We compromise the integrity of a friendship
when, through a fear of being unacceptable to another,
we fail to share our feelings.

UNREALISTIC AND HIDDEN EXPECTATIONS OF THE OTHER

Just as unrealistic expectations of ourselves can cripple
us, just as they may even paralyze us, so can our
unrealistic expectations of another make it impossible for
us to be a friend to that person.

The starting place in relationships is in ourselves. If
we know and understand ourselves, if we have an
awareness of our own strengths and limitations, and if we
set this in the context of God's love and acceptance of us,
then we will be less likely to impose on ourselves or
another a set of unexpressed expectations that can only
destroy a friendship.

Often in failed friendships, when we listen carefully
to someone who is struggling to understand what happened, if we ask, "Did you know this about that person?"
the answer is, "Yes, I knew it before we tried to be
friends, but I thought he'd change," "Yes, I knew this
but I thought that if she cared enough for me, she would
change." When we carry hidden expectations, friendship
becomes a plan to change another's life. Friendship
becomes the way we seek to transform another into a person who does things, says things, feels just the way we do.
We measure the love another has for us by that person's
willingness to follow not his own life agenda but ours. The
test of such a friendship becomes changing another rather
than accepting the special gift that the other is.

Our hidden or unrealistic expectations of someone
we call "friend" reflect our own sometimes hidden insecurities. We are afraid when another does not feel or

think or talk like us. We are afraid to stand alone and so we need this person, this friend, to be like us. Without realizing it, we may seek to destroy or change the only gift a friend has to give to us—the gift of a self that is different and unique.

Different sets of feelings for men and women

When, as men and women, we are free of the bondage that deprives us of a full and functional set of human feelings, we may be able to approach one another in friendship and with sensitivity. Whether by nature or nurture, men and women in our culture accept and operate out of different sets of feelings. The cultural stereotype of the male as the aggressor and the initiator of friendship and sexual sharing is no more destructive than the seductive female who cries "sexist" at every possible opportunity. A woman who has developed strong mothering instincts and who then mothers a man she says she loves is no less responsible for the ending of a friendship than a man who does not express his feelings to someone he says he loves because he has learned that a good man cannot have feelings of inadequacy and insecurity. For every woman who has accepted and shared her tears, there is a man who has been denied the healing experience of crying. For every man who has learned too well the value of being strong and independent, there is a woman who has been shown only the way of dependence.

Men and women search for ways to reclaim the feelings that are lost. Together they must search for ways of approaching another in friendship without which they cannot be good friends: men to men, women to women, and men and women to each other. The sexes do not have different or separate sets of feelings. The only way of being human is a way that passes through reclaiming feelings that have been denied or ignored to both women and men.

It is important to recognize the destructive elements in friendship. If cultural and personal patterns are to be changed, we need to scrutinize them carefully in order to give direction to that change.

It is equally important that we look for and identify those elements and qualities that make good friendship possible. We look to Jesus as our model as we respond to his invitation to "come and see" how he loved others.

Jesus' faithfulness to his Father's call and his faithfulness to himself were not separate in his life. The vision of life to which he responded grew out of the values that fashioned his personal integrity. The message of his life and of the Christian Gospel is that we cannot separate faithfulness to self, others and God. Unless I believe in myself, I have nothing to give to another. Unless I believe in God, I may not have the courage to pursue the difficult path to self-discovery. Unless I believe that I cannot live and grow in isolation, I will not follow the costly call to friendship.

Friendship finds its fullest expression in those who are able to both give and receive. The same Jesus who restores sight to the blind receives water from the woman at Jacob's well in Samaria. The public Jesus who responds to the demands of the crowds receives the vision of the little children who come to him. The Jesus who challenges all he meets to resist the power of evil listens to the tempter's deceptive appeals. The same Jesus who listens to Peter's tender words, "Lord, to whom shall we go?" challenges an overbearing Peter with "Get behind me, Satan."

The Jesus who calls the crowds to a new way of living accepts hospitality from a repentant tax collector. The Jesus who cries out against the sins of the flesh is ministered to by a woman of the street. The Jesus who is about to suffer and die gives and receives bread at the last meal he will share with his friends. That Jesus calls us to be aware of ways of giving in friendship that can only oppress when they are not accompanied by an openness to receive.

The greatest gift from God and the most important gift we give to one another is not the gift of love but the gift of freedom. Without this gift we cannot love God or one another. Friendship that is not freeing is not loving but enslaving. The gift of freedom makes it possible for us to discover, even through our darkness and sinfulness, the goodness and strength that are in us. Unless we are free to choose what is sinful and destructive, we can neither choose nor embrace what is grace-filling and life-giving. Jesus established special bonds with those who, having been enslaved by the way of selfishness and sin, now find the full life that is the heritage of those who understand what it means to be free.

The disciples who approached Jesus with the simple question, "Master, where do you live?" could not, at the moment, have understood the costly grace that would be needed to respond to his simple invitation to "come and see."

Like the child Eric, we are afraid of the darkness we experience as we search for the qualities in ourselves and others that are vital to friendship. Like him we know our own needs for companions "with skin on." We learn slowly, and we hear only a part of the message at any given time. We are discouraged by our own lack of vision and we are wounded by the darkness of others. We will grow weary and may even abandon the way of friendship unless we recognize that every effort to love, however frail and unseeing, is in itself an act of friendship. Every commitment to find the strength in our fragility is to grow stronger. When we look deep inside of ourselves in an effort to lessen the darkness there, we see more when we look out to others. Every time we reach out to another to accept the gift of friendship we return to our own inner journey with renewed light and life. And every such act of love finds its source in the God who is love.

St. Paul, in speaking to us of the imperfect love which we know all too well, reminds us that even imperfect love is a place where we know and are known. He invites us to recognize and even cherish the pitfalls to loving, for they call us to an ever more committed way of being friends to those with whom we share life. He reminds us that, of the few things that remain, love is the greatest. To be able to offer a gift of friendship that has been refined and freed of its destructive qualities is, indeed, to offer the greatest of gifts.

8 The symbols of friendship

> Something which has existed since the beginning,
> that we have heard,
> and we have seen with our own eyes;
> that we have watched and touched with our hands:
> the Word, who is life—
> this is our subject.
>
> *1 John 1:1*

Each person's journey of self-discovery unfolds in mysterious and unique ways. As we reflect on any part of the way we have come, we see more clearly not only the past but also the way that lies ahead. Every decision that has significance in our lives reveals to us not only who we are but who we can become.

The objects with which we surround ourselves, the pictures on our walls, and the books on our shelves reveal who we are. They also tell us something about who we will be. I remember waiting in the living room of a person I had not met before. Seeing books on his shelves by some of my favorite authors—Eliot, Frost, Rilke and Hammarskjold—prepared me well for the brief conversation we were to have.

One night at a social gathering a small group of us played a game called "The Ungame." Initially one of the group voiced his reservations about completing statements like "If I could be an animal I would choose to be . . . ," "If I could be any flower, I would wish to be . . . ," "If I could be any famous person who has ever lived, I would choose to be . . . ." As we were leaving the party, that same person said to me, "I am amazed at how much I learned about myself and everyone in that group. That game is for real.''

Each of us tells everyone we meet something about ourselves by the clothes we wear, the colors we favor, the music we enjoy, the books we read, the forms of relaxation we choose, the movies we attend. We also learn something about ourselves each time we notice or reflect on what we continue to choose. These choices that are apparent to ourselves and others are one kind of symbol telling us something about who we are and who we are becoming.

Carl Jung says that symbols are natural and spontaneous. They are not the conscious ways in which we give direction to our lives. It is not as though we plan to design a symbol for self. Jung says further that ''When we attempt to understand symbols, we are not only confronted with the symbol itself, but we are brought up against the wholeness of the symbol-producing individual.''

It has been said that the poet and the artist are like the direction-finders for the human family. They provide symbols for human experience long before we are able to verbalize the experience for ourselves. Through symbols we grow to greater insight in understanding and finding meaning in our lives. Even though we may not be able to verbalize or interpret the meaning, the symbol becomes a place of revelation for each of us.

In a poem called ''Revelation'' Robert Frost says that ''all who hide too well away/Must speak and tell us where they are.'' These words remind us that the expression of self is the first step in discovering and interpreting our lives to ourselves. The symbol reveals more than we are able to understand. The meaning of the symbol is far richer than our conscious self can comprehend.

We reveal ourselves to one another in the names we give and receive. A nickname we give to a friend tells something of what we know about that friend. It also says something about us because it reflects what we notice in another. Naming someone places us in a position of vulnerability because it reveals who we are by the very act of telling someone else who they are to us. When lovers are good friends the names they have for one another are symbols of openness and commitment. When lovers are not good friends, names may reveal the destructiveness or selfishness that typifies the relationship.

When we know enough of ourselves and another to call that person "friend" we have already discovered something about ourselves in relationship to that other person. We gradually come to know friends by telling them who they are to us.

When someone tells us what it means for us to be a friend, we look at our lives through eyes that see differently from our own. Our world is larger because it is then reflected through the eyes of another. We deprive one another of some of life's best gifts when we fail to tell each other what we see and how we feel. God calls us to life through the vision of life that is the gift of a friend.

So profound is the hidden meaning of some symbols that it may take us a lifetime to discover their fullest meaning. It is mysterious that we choose to express ourselves through the use of symbols that come to have a deeper meaning than we had ever envisioned. Certainly, in every friendship the meaning of the most common of symbols, such as a kiss or tender touch or embrace, grows as the friendship deepens through faithfulness and mutuality.

In failed or broken friendships one person may feel betrayed when someone distorts the meaning of a symbol by sharing it with one for whom it was never intended. A sacred symbol such as a ring or medallion that has been given as a sign of commitment and is accepted by the other becomes a source of pain if it is removed or replaced. Just as the acceptance once symbolized faithful sharing, so the removal of that symbol now becomes a pain-filled reminder of the deterioration or the end of a relationship. It is a reminder that, subconsciously, the symbol may have had a different meaning for the giver and the receiver at the time the gift was given.

In every experience of giving or receiving symbols, we can learn something about friendship that enriches every other friendship that we have. This will not just happen. It asks of us a spirit that is determined to notice what life is saying to us. It asks of us an openness to discover the new life that is present in the happy life-giving symbol and in the painful life-initiating one.

The Jesus who was touched and seen by others—the Jesus who gave and received friendship—that same Jesus calls us to cherish the symbols of life as rich sources of meaning. He gives us the example of a prayerful life, a life that sought time and space in which to listen to and reflect on the deep meaning present in even the most ordinary of life's circumstances. The Word made flesh spoke to us of the lilies of the field, the birds of the air, the mustard seed, the lost sheep, the house built on rock. He spoke of bread broken and of wine shared. He used the earthiest of images, the most ordinary examples, to remind us that our lives are rooted in this earth and that the meaning of life is to be found not in the heavens but here on earth. He invites us to express this life in human symbols that call us to life even as they express the meaning of life already discovered and shared.

The direction and meaning of my own life, the relationships with friends, and sense of God's presence with us always are deeply related to and inseparable from a set of personal symbols. The meaning of these symbols grows and changes as they help us interpret our lives to ourselves and others. One symbol is more important than all the others. Its meaning encompasses that of all the others.

THE DRIFTWOOD CROSS

The Mississippi River widens at Lake City, Minnesota, to form a lovely lake that is called Lake Pepin. My earliest roots in Minnesota, and my later roots in Wisconsin which is just across the river, have endeared this part of the country to me.

A friend who was teaching in Wisconsin invited me to spend time with her at the cabin of friends. As we walked the shores of Lake Pepin my eyes were attentive to the pieces of driftwood that had been washed up onto the beach. The shape and firmness of one piece were unusual. Because it had been lying on the beach it was bleached and weatherworn. The two pieces of wood that had grown together formed a nearly symmetrical cross. At the point where the two roots had grown together there was a woody knot, adding to the beauty of the grain and to the meaning of the symbol.

I did not think about that cross which I carried home and carefully tucked away until a special person came into my life. When I thought about some gift that I could give to that friend, a gift treasured by me, I began to sand, treat and polish the wood. Each new application of wax prepared this gift for my friend. It would be a symbol of our shared commitment to the Gospel and to life.

The gift was given and its meaning took on added significance for me when my friend called my attention to a passage in Chesterton's *Orthodoxy*. In speaking of Christianity and the cross he says:

As we have taken the circle as the symbol of reason and madness, we may very well take the cross as the symbol at once of mystery and of health. Buddhism is centripetal, but Christianity is centrifugal: it breaks out. For the circle is perfect and infinite in its nature; but it is fixed for ever in its size; it can never be larger or smaller. But the cross, though it has at its heart a collision and a contradiction, can extend its four arms for ever without altering its shape. Because it has a paradox in its centre it can grow without changing. The circle returns upon itself and is bound. The cross opens its arms to the four winds; it is a signpost for free travellers.[1]

Not only did the gift I gave my friend receive new meaning through the words of Chesterton, its meaning has deepened through several years. A symbol that seemed so simple and clear in the giving and in the receiving has continued to take on a meaning I had never envisioned. It has reflected the meaning of faithfulness to friendship and to Christianity in more ways than I have sometimes cared to know.

As I think of the meaning of that gift now, I recognize it as a direction-finder for my own life. The symbolic meaning of that piece of wood which I embraced that day on the shore of Lake Pepin now reaches into my life. That driftwood cross is a continual reminder that the best gifts of life and the most terrible experiences of pain are never far apart. God has a way of calling us to accountability for the words we use and the symbols through which we express our search for life and friendship. God's love calls us from the surface of what we express to the deeper challenge of owning the meaning of

[1] G. K. Chesterton, *Orthodoxy* (Garden City: Doubleday Image, 1959), p. 14.

the symbols through which we express both friendship and life.

On some days, when I think of what that gift meant at the giving, I think of Robert Frost's final statement in "The Oven Bird": "The question that he frames in all but words/Is what to make of a diminished thing."

And then I remember Chesterton's challenge to believe that the cross is a symbol of growing endlessly, without limit, without restriction. The driftwood cross calls me to enflesh my own symbol. The growing meaning of that cross encompasses all of the other symbols that are important to me.

Jesus, the Word made flesh, continually calls our attention to the symbolic value of all that surrounds us. Jesus tells us to look at what we see and to come to an understanding of the realities that we do not see:

> Take the fig tree as a parable: as soon as its twigs grow supple and its leaves come out, you know that summer is near. So with you when you see all these things: know that he is near, at the very gates.
>
> *Matthew 24: 32-33*

In the Gospels, Jesus invites us to take notice of the symbols through which we express ourselves. Deepening our understanding of the symbols that are ours is an important way of recognizing who we are. Symbols are an irreplaceable channel, giving direction to our lives. Unless we reflect on our symbols, we may miss the meaning in our lives.

The symbols of life and of friendship differ for each of us. Some of them are rooted in the Hebrew Scriptures, some in the Word of God, and some in the word of our own lives. Reflecting on symbols that are important to us and sharing them with others is one way of growing to a new and ever deeper understanding of their meaning.

THE RAINBOW

When someone first pointed out to me that the rainbow was a symbol of God's faithful love for us, it gave new meaning to a rainbow pendant a friend had given me. Reading and reflecting on the meaning of the words in Genesis 9 has deepened the value of my friend's gift. It has expanded my vision of God's love and of the meaning of faithful friendship.

> God said, "Here is a sign of the Covenant I make between myself and you and every living creature with you for all generations: I set my bow in the clouds and it shall be a sign of the Covenant between me and the earth. When I gather the clouds over the earth and the bow appears in the clouds, I will recall the Covenant between myself and you and every living creature of every kind."
> *Genesis 9: 12-15*

The rainbow, like our lives together, is grounded in the earth. It is a reminder that the God who loves us, the God who sent the Word made flesh to be our companion and friend, calls us to find life by being friends to one another.

The colors of the rainbow, like the colors of our lives and the colors of friendship, range from bright hues to darker tones. They are a reminder that every color reflects life and friendship, that every color is important to the fabric of our human existence. Just as the rainbow reminds us of God's faithful love for us so does it call us to be faithful friends to one another.

Shopkeepers have discovered that the rainbow is a marketable item. There are rainbow shops in malls. We see rainbows on billboards, on roadside signs, and on gasoline storage tanks. What a tragedy if those of us who take God's word seriously allow this symbol to be lost to our lives by allowing it to become just another multicolored marketable item.

THE BRIDGE

The Latin word for priest is *pontifex*. It means "bridge-builder," "one who makes connections between things."

—Bridges, like the rainbow, are grounded in the earth.

—Bridges are like open lifelines bringing food and shelter. They carry people to one another.

—Bridges are symbols of faithfulness. They promise to be there when we need them. Sometimes we understand what a bridge means only when a bridge on which we rely is destroyed.

—Bridges are symbols of human creativity. They are built of every possible material and out of a great variety of designs.

—Bridges are not selective. Bridge-keepers may be, but bridges are not. They allow us to walk on them or to drive over them to get to a place that is important to us.

—Bridges are symbols for friendship. Like Jesus, our priest, our "bridge over troubled water," bridges help us to understand that there is no life in isolation. Everything that has life is somehow connected to all life. What the poet says of Jesus is asked of each of us in relationship to one another:

> One who was Bridge himself
> Broken and torn in spanning that long way
> From man to God—
> One who will always come
> Ten thousand miles
> To our one step—
> Embraces you at last,
> You who have spent your life
> To make us understand
> That every life is needing to be met.

Now you have crossed that Bridge alone
That spans eternity
To carry man to God[2]

Hands

Human hands have been the subject of the artist's brush
and the poet's pen. Hands and our underdeveloped sense
of touch have served as the topic for workshops and for
communication seminars.

Palm readers study the lines in hands and seek to
reveal more of life to the person who listens. Hands tell us
something of a person's occupation, they speak to us of
gentleness or of violence. But, nowhere do hands speak to
us with greater importance than in friendship.

The open hands of a friend reach out to tell us that
we are welcome and that there is a place for us. To open
our hands to another is to be vulnerable to that person
because in extending our hands and ourselves to another
we risk being rejected.

Gentle hands heal us and bring new strength and
hope. They tell us that the person who touches us wishes
to share life with us. Because gentle hands are not ex-
ploitive, we feel cherished when they touch us.

Strong hands bring support and courage. When we
are discouraged or sad our spirit is lifted up by the offer of
such hands.

Hands extended in friendship are like the hands of
which Teilhard de Chardin speaks:

. . . And I've come to think that the only, the supreme,
prayer we can offer up during these hours when the
road before us is shrouded in darkness, is that of our
Master on the cross: "In manus tuas commendo
spiritum." (Into your hands I commend my spirit.) To

[2] Sister Helen Delores Sweeney, "For John Berryman."

the hands that broke and gave life to the bread, that blessed and caressed, that were pierced; to the hands that are as our hands, of which we can never say what they will do with the objects they hold, whether shatter them or care for them, but whose whims, we may be sure, are full of kindness and will never do more than hold us close in a jealous grasp—to the kindly and mighty hands that reach down to the very marrow of the soul—that mould and create—to the hands through which so great a love is transmitted—it is to these that it is good to surrender our soul, above all when we suffer or are afraid. And in so doing there is a great happiness and great merit. So, let us do so together.[3]

SYMBOLS FOR GOD

Because the love of God and others can never be separated, so the symbols through which we express friendship have meaning for the threefold relationship with self, others and God that permeates all of human life. As the meaning of each symbol for God grows so does the realization of the ways in which it touches all relationships.

Teilhard's meditation took on a new meaning for me when a friend gave me a slide of the work of Milles, a Swedish sculptor. This work is called "The Hand of God." The artist portrays a very large hand at the top of a tall pillar. Poised on the hand, in a stance of trust and openness, is the figure of a man.

It is important for me to know that there is a Presence in my life who cares for me always. A Presence who gives vision when my own is not clear. A Presence who stays with me whether I walk in certainty and light or in uncertainty and darkness. A Presence who calls me to

[3] Teilhard de Chardin, *The Making of a Mind* (New York: Harper and Row, 1965).

life in surprising and painful ways. A Presence to whom I reach when my own strength and courage are not enough.

Sustained and loved by this Presence who is God, I stand in openness and trust in relation to my own life and future. Led by this Presence, called to life by this Presence, I respond with a courage that is greater than my own. Loved by this Presence, I have more love to share with those with whom I make my human journey.

"The Hand of God," the artist Milles called his work. It is a symbol that remains an ongoing reminder of who God is for me.

At a retreat weekend for the handicapped which I volunteered to help staff, we were asked to take clay and form our symbol for God. The sharing of those symbols remains with me. Those symbols expand my own.

A 23-year-old man, a cerebral palsy victim, made a door. He said that he feels confined and closed in because he often cannot get to places he'd like to be. An open door is his image of a God who calls him to life, a God who does not limit him in ways that the people he meets sometimes do.

A young woman who was barely ambulatory made a foot. She said that God leads her to life, that God is like a healthy foot that is not limited.

A teenage boy with a body devastated by polio made a flower. He said that God is all the beauty in the world. He likes flowers because they bring beauty into his life just as God does.

A blind woman's symbol was an anchor. She said that she trusts God and relies on him for strength.

A young girl paralyzed by a car accident made a happy face. She said that she knows God loves her and smiles on her always.

The symbols of those who had some physical disabili

ty were much more creative and concrete than were those of the rest of us.

I was reminded of the ways in which images of God that are not faithful to who God is, continue to plague us. Some such symbols of God are of a computer who keeps a count of good and bad deeds, a vending machine that dispenses gifts if our input is proper, a trap that lies in wait for our sinfulness to show itself, and a tough disciplinarian who calls us to task for our errant ways.

Each of these is an image of a god that is not God. None of these reflects the God who, in Genesis, says, "The rainbow in the heavens is a reminder of my ever-present love."

Karl Barth tells us that we Christians have followed the false image of the "God of the therefore." Faithfulness to God's love and to our lives demands that we replace that god with our Christian God who says, "Yes, you have failed, you have sinned, you have made mistakes, you did not see the harm you would do, *nevertheless* I will always love you." We are called to be *nevertheless* people in friendship.

The clown

In our time when the traditional circus clown is, unfortunately, nearly an extinct species, there is a whole new cult of clowns and clowning. Like the rainbow and the butterfly, the people who understand the dynamics of commercialism want to make the clown their own.

"The Parable," a film that portrayed the Christ figure as a clown, was praised by some and condemned by others. I remember walking out of a performance of "Godspell" just ahead of a woman who was loudly proclaiming the production "blasphemous and disrespectful, destructive of all religion."

We are out of touch with a tradition in the circus that knew of the one call that could calm the crowds in times of tragedy. That call was, "Send in the clowns." It was recognized that the clown, like no other presence in the circus community, could minister to and heal a hurting or troubled crowd. The clown was not looked upon as just another funny person. The clown embodied the human experience of both comedy and tragedy in such a way as to transform each. The symbol of the clown is an important link between our love of God and our love for each other in friendship:

> The art of clowning is the humane art in which man finds his way to the center, the definite place at which God promises to meet him. It taps resources of which tragedy, for all its insight and nobility, is ignorant. Knowing he is a fool, the clown chooses to act the part and so discovers a pattern of truth. If he responds to that pattern and opens his life to the power of the clown with passion, it is called faith. If through laughter he serves his fellows and shares their lot, it is called love. If he moves toward God as the Joy of the present and future, it is called hope. So faith, love, hope affirm the pattern and commend it to others. The jesting spirit has been loosed among us; who can resist it?[4]

Conclusion

We are a symbol-making people. We are a symbol-receiving people. Unless we are also a prayerful, self-reflective people we will miss not only the meaning of our symbols, but we will be denied the most complete experience of human life. Since we do not discover the varied meanings of any symbol in isolation from others, we are also a symbol-sharing people.

[4] Joseph C. McClelland, *The Clown and the Crocodile* (Richmond: John Knox Press, 1970), p. 119.

It is only in friendship that the meaning of human life can be interpreted and understood. Because we do not live and grow in isolation the meaning of symbols, like the meaning of our human experience, unfolds gradually and only when it is shared.

Symbols that seem to enter our lives in a nearly un-noticed way can grow to a place of unexpected significance. Symbols that seem to enter from the margins and surface places of our lives often become central and inner-directed. Those that enter from the outside in can grow and deepen only from the inside out.

Like the driftwood cross whose meaning reaches out to embrace every other symbol that I hold dear, so does God enrich our lives when we open ourselves to and receive all that we can see and watch and touch. Like Jesus, we are called to be God's Word made flesh. Like Jesus, God's Word and the word of our lives are made flesh in us only in friendship.

9 Life in the ruins: Finding meaning in failed friendship

> We are only the earthenware jars that hold this treasure, to make it clear that such an overwhelming power comes from God and not from us. We are in difficulties on all sides, but never cornered; we see no answer to our problems, but never despair; we have been persecuted, but never deserted; knocked down, but never killed; always, wherever we may be, we carry with us in our body the death of Jesus, so that the life of Jesus, too, may always be seen in our body.
>
> *2 Corinthians 4:7-10*

THERE IS a traditional Hebrew tale about an old farmer who went out into his field. He worked in the field and then could not return to his home because it was the sabbath. When he returned to his village his Rabbi said to the old man, "Did you pray while you were in the field over sabbath?" The farmer looked at the Rabbi and said, "Rabbi, you know that I am not a learned man. You know that I do not know the sacred prayers. I could not pray while I was in the field." The Rabbi then asked, "What did you do through all those long hours while you were in the field over the sacred sabbath?" The old man said, "I could only recite the letters of the alphabet and ask God to form them into something that has meaning."

The old farmer was wiser than he knew. His story has a meaning that speaks to every human life, for each of us stands before God carrying with us the alphabet of our human experience. The letters of our alphabet bear differing names. Some of the letters of the experience of every life are named success and failure, joy and sadness, friendship and isolation, love and rejection. Some letters are named security, others insecurity; some goodness and

131

others sinfulness. Every letter of each human alphabet is sacred and cherished by God because we are. Every human experience carries with it God's call to life. No human experience is the end of all life, though many human experiences are the end of some dimension of life. Every letter that signals an end calls us to some new beginning. This is equally true for the end of a relationship and for the end of one season of a relationship.

When we come before God, when we offer him the alphabet that is ours, it is as though we sort the letters and offer God only one portion of our lives. With confidence we offer him the letters that are named success and joy and love. We offer him our experience of security and goodness. Because it is so difficult for us to accept failure and sadness and rejection, because we cannot forgive ourselves for our insecurity and sinfulness, we are sometimes afraid to offer these letters of life. God is not the problem, we are. God does not ask of us a perfect record; we impose it on ourselves.

The old farmer was wiser than we are. He recited the letters of the alphabet, all of them, each of them. He relied on God to make sense of what was nonsense to him. He trusted that God could shape meaning that he could not find.

The old farmer lived close to the meaning of God's promise of faithfulness to those who love and follow the call to life:

> Should you pass through the sea, I will be
>   with you;
> or through rivers, they will not swallow
>   you up.
> Should you walk through fire, you will not
>   be scorched
> and the flames will not burn you.
> For I am Yahweh, your God.   *Isaiah 43:2-3*

One of the great dangers in rejecting a certain set of our experiences is that we may become spectators rather than participants in life. Those who set out to avoid failure and rejection and criticism and all the other pain-filled letters that are a part of life can do so only by choosing to avoid life itself.

In Thornton Wilder's play, *The Angel That Troubled the Waters,* we witness a dialog between an invalid and a physician, both of whom have come to the pool to be healed. The wise physician knows and accepts his need for healing, a need not as obvious as that of the invalid. The invalid recognizes the physician as one who has healed members of his own family. He argues that one who heals surely does not need a place in the pool. The invalid refuses to accept in the physician what the physician was able to accept in himself. The healing angel approaches the pool and speaks to the physician:

> Without your wounds where would your power be? It is your very remorse that makes your low voice tremble into the hearts of men. The very angels themselves cannot persuade the wretched and blundering children on earth as can one human being broken in the wheels of living. In Love's service only the wounded soldiers can serve. Physician, draw back.[1]

We understand the words of the angel when we take time to reflect on the qualities we expect in those we seek counsel or understanding from when we are bruised or in need. We understand these words when we reflect on the life of Jesus and take time to notice how he was wounded by criticism, misunderstanding, insensitivity and the rejection even of his friends. St. Paul tells us that the letters of the alphabet of Jesus' experience were like ours in every way except sin.

We have a natural fear of endings that we have not

[1] Thornton Wilder, *The Angel That Troubled the Waters* (New York: Coward McCann Co., 1931).

chosen. We find it difficult to believe that there is a renewal of love possible for us in being rejected by someone we love. Who of us would not choose success over failure as a way to life? But, when we take a more than superficial look at the roots of new life and at the growing edges of our own experience, we discover again that places of pain are also places of life. There is life in the ruins. It is life waiting to be discovered and chosen.

We find stories of courage in unexpected places. We find heroes whose lives help us believe that where others have walked, we, too, can walk. John Heagle, in his book, *Our Journey Toward God,* says that "A hero is someone who goes someplace where no one else has ever been." We are all heroes as we walk in love and friendship into unknown territory. We are all heroes through God's ongoing call to life.

I read a story about a man named Roger Reynolds, who jumps from airplanes. A few years ago, he jumped carrying two parachutes. As his body travelled through the air at a speed of 90 miles per hour, his first parachute failed to open and when the second one did open it became entangled in the first. He landed in a wooded area and was later taken to a nearby hospital. He broke 14 major bones in his body.

The story went on to say that, since that tragic accident, he has jumped 100 times, has run the Boston Marathon twice, and is now studying medicine at the Indiana University Medical School. He plans to be an orthopedic surgeon. This man's courage took him far beyond his own personal recovery. It led him to a desire to share the life that he had rescued from his personal tragedy by helping others as he was helped. How different the ending to his story might have been had he not somehow known that in every ending is an invitation to a new beginning.

Someone has described life as living between two trapezes. To see beyond the place we know, to have the courage to let go of that secure place is the only way we have of coming to a new place of life. We may refuse to leave what we know for what we do not know. Sam Keen says that "It is in the empty spaces that new things begin" but we have no certitude as to what those new things will be.

Each time we are secure enough to risk dealing with insecurity, we strengthen our ability to risk life for new and richer life. We cannot get to that second trapeze, that place of new life, unless we let go knowing full well that we have no certainty that every risk will bring the life we seek. We can let go knowing, with certainty, that there will be another trapeze, another decision, another choice for life.

The greatest risks we take, the risks that ask the most of us are those that are present in every effort to give and receive friendship. Just as there is no joy equal to that of receiving the love of a good and faithful friend, so there is no suffering that can equal failing and being failed by a friend. The greatest tragedy in this failure would be to have learned nothing.

Failure in friendship may be final. When it is final, it may very well be that neither friend noticed signs all along the way that could have told them some painful truths about the patterns both were setting. If these signs go unnoticed, for whatever reason, a precious gift may reach a place where either or both of the friends may choose not to make the personal investment necessary to go on.

In friendships between men and women, it most often is the woman who first senses some area of the relationship that needs attention. She may be able neither to understand clearly nor to verbalize what her instincts tell her. But she will speak of what she is feeling. She may even suggest that they seek help. A man, not noticing what she has, may either refuse to examine what she sees or reject her suggestion that someone else could help them.

Two people set the patterns in a friendship; two people choose the gift. One person cannot sustain a friendship nor can one person resolve a difficulty. What comes to be a problem area for one person is a problem for both and must not be too easily dismissed. All too often what one person could not understand at a given point is clear much later. It may be too late to save that friendship.

The point of failure in a friendship, even if not final, is painful because it requires both people to examine carefully what had before gone unnoticed. It is another painful process of self-discovery. It is an opportunity for renewed and greater life in a friendship if both friends are willing to let go of the security of the first trapeze and move on to a new level of friendship that might never have been discovered without having come upon this costly growing edge of the relationship.

Each friend grows when each is able to look beyond the ways in which they have been hurt by someone else to a place where both recognize and accept responsibility for the pain and for the new direction it can give. It is no simple or comfortable process to let go of seeing the harm done to us and to grow to a place of taking responsibility for having hurt someone we called "friend."

We are not speaking here of deliberate hurt, though that is also possible. We are speaking of the subconscious and undiscovered regions of self which too often determine our way of giving and receiving friendship. We are influenced though not controlled by ways of relating that were first modelled for us by our parents or guardians. We are influenced by the cultural patterns of society. We are influenced by literature and poetry, as writers depict for us, through the lives of fictional people, what friendship is and what it means for human life. Long before we have made conscious decisions about the values we bring to friendship and relationships, we have a storehouse of inner recorded data that will influence our choices.

Nowhere more than in friendship are we aware of the meaning of St. Paul's words when he says that we are fragile, that we carry the treasure of each other's life in earthen vessels. No place in life is more sacred and more vulnerable than the place where friends meet to share life. No other place is at once both a place of singularly beautiful happiness and terrifyingly pain-filled sadness as is friendship.

Coming to understand our own way of being a friend is a long and gradual process. The process can be helped by cherishing what we learn from each friendship as it relates to every other friend that we have.

We are not born with good friendship skills. We are not presented with some gift of facility in identifying or expressing our feelings. We are badly wounded by cultural programming about the acceptability of expressing different sets of feelings as men and women.

Self-revelation can only happen at the rate at which we continue to learn more about ourselves. Sharing what we learn with someone else places us in a position of possible hurt. We will never face any form of rejection if we develop masterful skills in hiding from everyone we meet. We will face the ultimate form of rejection because we cannot hide and come to know and love ourselves. Only in friendship can we cherish the beauty given to us by God and revealed to us through the eyes of a friend.

But, there is more than beauty and goodness in us. And a friend who is faithful will reveal to us that which is neither beautiful nor good. A good friend reveals this not to make us less than we are but to invite us to become more.

Yeats says that "Only a shock resulting from the greatest possible conflict can make the greatest possible change." It is unfortunate that we too often choose to avoid the conflict and, at a greater cost, are hidden from the opportunity to make the life-giving change. We grieve for the pain of final failure in friendship that is not life-giving. What a terrible thing it is to experience the final failure of a friendship and then lack the courage to search in the ruins for the keys to new life. We may be too vulnerable and bruised to do this unless we have the support and love of other friends.

Christians have the gift of the life of Jesus. When we see the stories of his life not as his alone, but as reflections of our lives, then we have some way of objectifying the rejection we have felt, the forms of betrayal that we have known or feared, the harsh criticism that cuts deep. When we look carefully at the life of Jesus we also find there the hope and the source of renewed life that only friendship brings. At one time or another, the death and resurrection of Jesus will be reflected in every faithful friendship. We miss his message if we look for one without the other. We miss the meaning of the Hebrew tale unless we understand that we do not have full life unless we accept and cherish both.

God's call to life does not make of us everlasting interior excavators. The call to find life in the ruins is no invitation to remain in that place of failure. The journey to life asks that we settle forever into neither the place of failure nor the place of comfort. The journey through failure to renewed life, like the death and resurrection of Jesus, is a journey that is repeated many times in the life of every faithful man and woman. As we look in the ruins we must remember that we will not find all of life in any one place. Some of life will be discovered at another time and in another way. Faithfulness to God's call to life asks us to risk trusting not only the friend who walks with us, but the Source of all love and life. We cannot do everything, but we must do our part. God will not do what we must do, but he can and will do what only one who is Love itself can do.

God remains with us throughout the journey. He loves and accepts us in ways no other friend can or will. His invitation to life, unlike that of any other friend, unites the call and the promise of fulfilling that call. The life he gives can grow only by being shared.

Like the old Hebrew farmer we stand before God with only the gift of the letters of the alphabet of our lives. In our reluctance to accept the letters that remind us of the ways in which we have failed ourselves and others, we can hope for the acceptance from God that will help us find the meaning that is inevitably there. We hope that we, like the physician, will not only recognize our need for healing but cherish it for the life-giving gift it is. We pray with St. Paul that the ''overwhelming power that comes from God'' will heal us and that friends who have been hurt by our inner darkness will forgive us.

We make many beginnings in friendship because we believe in it for ourselves and for others. We offer the best kind of friendship that we know, realizing sometimes too late that what we offered was not enough. We search for the signs of life that can be recovered from the ruins of a once meaningful friendship. We leave with a loving God what we cannot decipher. And, we go on.

> Home is where one starts from. As we grow older
> The world becomes stranger, the pattern more
>   complicated
> Of dead and living. Not the intense moment

Isolated, with no before and after,
But a lifetime burning in every moment
And not the lifetime of one man only
But of old stones that cannot be deciphered. . . .
In my end is my beginning.[1]

[1] T. S. Eliot, "East Coker," *The Complete Poems and Plays* (New York: Harcourt, Brace and World, 1971), p. 129.

10 Faithfulness: The meaning of commitment

> But because of Christ, I have come to consider all these advantages that I had as disadvantages. . . . For him I have accepted the loss of everything, and I look on everything as so much rubbish if only I can have Christ and be given a place in him. . . . All I want is to know Christ and the power of his resurrection. . . . Not that I have become perfect yet: I have not yet won. . . . All I can say is that I forget the past and I strain ahead for what is still to come; I am racing for the finish, for the prize to which God calls us upwards to receive in Christ Jesus. . . . Let us go forward on the road that has brought us to where we are.
>
> *Philippians 3: 7-16*

I REMEMBER that afternoon in Minneapolis as though it were yesterday. I had spent most of the day working with a friend in the kitchen of a small duplex that was located beside a large, open field. As we took a few moments from our work I looked out the kitchen window and, much to my surprise, saw a deer near the middle of the field.

Not trusting what I saw, I called to my friend. The deer that we saw was frantic, running here and there, seeming at once desperate and dangerous.

As I watched this creature confined, not by wall or fence but by its own survival patterns, I was terrified. I thought of the rush hour traffic about to begin on an expressway only three blocks away. I thought of the heavy traffic on University Avenue one block from where we were. I wondered if this beautiful animal would harm itself or cause a multivehicle accident in its efforts to find a familiar place. I wondered where it had come from and how it had gotten into the heart of the city.

141

In a few brief moments, the animal darted behind the nearby bank building and was gone. My friend and I ran out into the field, but there was no sign of the deer. I do not know where it went. Late that evening I watched the news with the expectation of a reported accident but there was none.

Memories of that deer and that day came back to me a few weeks later when I was backpacking in the Big Horn Mountains in northeastern Wyoming. My companions and I had stopped for lunch beside a peaceful stream. As we sat there savoring our lemonade and instant soup, a deer approached the stream in search of water. We were just a few feet away. The deer turned, looked at us, and then moved nearer the water and remained for several minutes. It somehow sensed that no harm would come to it here.

This graceful animal standing quietly near the water differed greatly from the deer that I saw in that city field. The memory of that frightened animal, imprisoned in the foreign land of a city, struggling to survive, haunted me. Its movements were jerky and awkward. In desperation, it had looked here and there for something in this environment that was familiar.

But the deer standing only a few feet from us, alternately enjoying the cool water and turning to look at us, was like the many other deer I've seen while backpacking. Sensing itself to be in a safe place, a place of shelter and protection, this deer was peaceful. Its movements were quietly gentle. When it did move, it gave the impression that this was home, here it felt secure.

The contrasts between those two animals have provided me with substantial food for long periods of personal reflection. Sometimes the basic image changes slightly, but most often it is the same. In that image there are not two separate deer, there are but two greatly differing life responses from the same animal.

It first seemed to me that the deer near the mountain stream was the "real" one and that the one in the field was not because most deer I have seen were peaceful and moved agilely. Something in me judged that the animal outside my house in the city was less "deerlike" because it was less like those I was familiar with.

The image of the two deer came to have clear meaning for me only when I saw in them two different and often unreconciled aspects of my own life. Like the deer I am sometimes secure and peaceful, other times fragile and frightened. I struggle to understand two such different and seemingly contradictory facets of my life. Faithfulness to my life challenges me to accept and reconcile the presence of two seemingly opposed aspects of my own life. Faithfulness to friendship involves me in the lives of others who seek the same inner reconciliation. Reconciling these is what Dietrich Bonhoeffer calls costly grace:

> Costly grace is the gospel which must be *sought* again and again, the gift which must be *asked* for, the door at which a man must knock.
>
> Such grace is *costly* because it calls us to follow, and it is *grace* because it calls us to follow *Jesus Christ*. It is costly because it costs a man his life, and it is grace because it gives a man the only true life. It is costly because it condemns sin, and grace because it justifies the sinner. Above all, it is *costly* because it cost God the life of his Son: "ye were bought at a price," and what has cost God much cannot be cheap for us. Above all, it is *grace* because God did not reckon his Son too dear a price to pay for our life, but delivered him up for us. Costly grace is the Incarnation of God.
>
> . . . Costly grace confronts us as a gracious call to

follow Jesus, it comes as a word of forgiveness to the
broken spirit and the contrite heart. Grace is costly
because it compels a man to submit to the yoke of
Christ and follow him; it is grace because Jesus says:
"My yoke is easy and my burden is light."[1]

None of us is born faithful. Each of us makes choices that
limit our freedom. The price of faithfulness is high. It cost
Jesus a criminal's death on the cross. The choices that
destroy our freedom can, for a long time, go unnoticed.
The pearl of faithfulness is purchased only at the high
price of discovering who we are because all faithfulness is
part of fidelity to self. The treasure of freedom is hidden in
counterfeits of rationalization and license which can only
enslave. Like the deer that strayed too far from an environment that was most conducive to its life and safety,
sometimes only tragedy signals to us that we are becoming less than we are because some inner darkness has
enslaved us.

Human faithfulness and freedom are not dimensions
of life which, once chosen, become forever ours. They are
forged out of the stuff of daily existence, fashioned in the
undramatic and unnoticed. That is why they stand the
chance of being lost without our noticing. Just as they can
be lost through a series of small choices made over a long
period of time, so are they reclaimed only in the same persistent manner. We miss the meaning of the Christian call
to conversion if we believe that it happens in one clear and
obvious moment. In his *Faust* Goethe says, "He only
earns his freedom and existence who daily conquers them
anew."

Faithfulness and freedom are inseparable. I feel
richly blessed by God to have had a father and a mother
who knew this. My parents who gave life to eight of us
never took that gift back.

[1] Dietrich Bonhoeffer, *The Cost of Discipleship* (New York: Macmillan, 1963), pp. 47-48.

All too often parents who give life to their children spend the rest of their lives taking it back bit by bit. A mother who allows the umbilical cord to be cut on the day of a child's birth may, by the time that child is grown, have grafted it back. Some children are less free at 20 than they were at birth. This is often especially true with a mother and a son, or a father and a daughter. Parents may try to continue to make decisions for their children.

A child, like any adult who is not set free to make decisions and not given a margin for error, is blocked from the way to faithfulness. We have set a higher value on never being hurt and not making mistakes than we have on life that is full only when it is both faithful and free.

Faithfulness and freedom do not come simply with the passage of time. Unfortunately, many senior citizens are neither faithful nor free. They are simply old. And some young people who have caught hold of their lives give testimony to the beauty of both faithfulness and freedom.

Because faithfulness and freedom are values that can become our own only through personal decision, we cannot make another person either faithful or free. We may be helpful by opening doors and by removing obstacles. We may encourage and affirm. We may love and support. We may question and challenge. But the decisions and the course to be followed for another person's life can never be ours.

Faithfulness and freedom are not something that we will have tomorrow. The choices we make today, the values that we choose today, these determine tomorrow. One of the great pitfalls for us as Christians is the future orientation that would have us believe that heaven is what matters and that earth is just a steppingstone. Our life after death is a continuation of our life now. Transforma-

tion takes place today and each day. We will be faithful
and free tomorrow only if we prize faithfulness and
freedom today.

I am reminded of Samuel Beckett's play, *Waiting for
Godot.* When Gogo and Didi, two gentlemen of the road,
are asked why they wait or what they are doing, they
always answer, "We are waiting for Godot." They
mistakenly believe that only after that meeting can life
have meaning for them. Meanwhile, life and all of its opportunities for friendship pass them by. Gogo continually
asks, "Tomorrow, how will I feel about today?" The
question he fails to ask, the question without which no life
has meaning is "What about today? Who are my friends
today?"

In *The Rose,* a film portraying the life of a rock star,
the tragic flaw is the same. She perceives as enemies her
agent, her public, her parents, and a man who tries to
love her. While distancing herself from all of them and
from her own life, she continues to say, "When I go home
to Florida, it will be different . . . After Florida . . ."
What was brought home dramatically by her ultimate
self-destruction was that "after Florida" could not be different unless she gave and received love each day.

Faithfulness and freedom are not qualities we ac-
quire for or because of someone else. We seek to become
faithful and free because, unless we do, we will be less
than we are. We seek to become faithful and free because
unless we do we cannot discover who we are and can
never give the gift we are to another. When we discover
this and believe it, we may be hurt by the unfaithfulness
of another but never destroyed. If we set out to be faithful
to another for another, then we will be angry and disappointed when that person's response does not seem pro-
portionate to our gift. Even if we set out to be faithful to
God for God, we may be angry when we suffer or when

we fail. Our faithfulness to God calls us to unlock the secret of who we are. Our faithfulness to God's gift calls us to free ourselves of all that would make us less than we are because unless we do, we will not be free. Our faithfulness to God is inseparable from our search for the meaning of faithfulness and freedom. Our ability to be a faithful friend to another depends on this search. For us as for our companion and brother Jesus, to be unfaithful to our values and commitments is ultimately to betray ourselves. St. Paul says of Jesus: "Here is a saying that you can rely on . . . We may be unfaithful, but he is always faithful, for he cannot disown his own self" (2 Tm 2:11,13).

Though a God who loves us continues to call us to faithfulness and freedom, that love does not depend on the unfailing constancy of our response. The images of God's faithfulness are as tender as that of a faithful husband who continues to love an unfaithful wife:

> Then she will say, "I will go back to my
>   first husband,
> I was happier then than I am today."
>
> That is why I am going to lure her
> and lead her out into the wilderness
> and speak to her heart. . . .
> There she will respond to me as she did
>   when she was young,
> as she did when she came out of the land
>   of Egypt.
>   *Hosea 2:13-15*

God's faithfulness is reassuring and life-giving. It brings prosperity and strength. It fortifies personal convictions:

> With my faithfulness and love,
> his fortunes shall rise in my name.
>
> I will keep my love for him always,
> my covenant with him shall stand.

> I will not break my covenant,
> I will not revoke my given word;
> I have sworn on my holiness, once for all and cannot
> turn liar to David.
>
> *Psalm 89: 24, 28,34-35*

God's faithfulness is like that of a loving parent. God's love for us began before we were born. It will be with us through each day of our life here. It will remain with us in the life that lies beyond this one. It challenges us to be faithful as God is:

> Yahweh called me before I was born,
> from my mother's womb he pronounced my name.
>
> Does a woman forget her baby at the breast,
> or fail to cherish the son of her womb?
> Yet even if these forget,
> I will never forget you.
>
> See, I have branded you on the palms
> of my hands.   *Isaiah 49:1,15-16*

God's faithfulness transforms even our weakness and sinfulness into goodness and life. For this reason, St. Paul boasts of his failures. He sees in them a gift that is at once humanizing and redeeming. He speaks of a gift that reassures us:

> To stop me from getting too proud I was given a thorn in the flesh, an angel of Satan to beat me and stop me from getting too proud! About this thing, I have pleaded with the Lord three times for it to leave me, but he has said, "My grace is enough for you: my power is at its best in weakness." So I shall be very happy to make my weaknesses my special boast so that the power of Christ may stay over me, and that is why I am quite content with my weaknesses, and with insults, hardships, persecutions, and the agonies I go through for Christ's sake. For it is when I am weak that I am strong.   *2 Corinthians 12: 7-10*

Like the peaceful deer beside the stream, we recognize and are drawn to people who have allowed God's faithfulness to touch their lives. We sense the goodness and inner beauty that accompany the continued difficult response to live a life that is both faithful and free. We know the price that Jesus paid.

The frightened deer is so like us as we struggle with fears and insecurities. It is not easy to walk in the companionship of Jesus. Faithfulness to a God who continually leads us to new life is a commitment that we can neither make nor keep easily. Friendships, necessary for life and growth, sometimes succeed and sometimes fail. We often pray for courage with wounded hearts and fragile hopes. The knowledge that someone has done it and that life can be fuller and richer after suffering does not necessarily bring light on a dark day. All the poetry about the paschal mystery and its meaning for Jesus does not bring us through every Good Friday to a bright Easter Sunday. We wonder, sometimes, if God might not have made some other mystery central to the Christian experience.

The memory of others who have walked the way we walk and who have shared the struggles we know brings us the message of God's love. Like St. Paul we pray for the courage to know Christ and, like him, to discover the life that accompanies every form of suffering and death.

11 Friendship and the Eucharist: The meaning of presence

> Then they told their story of what had happened on the road and how they had recognized him at the breaking of the bread.
>
> *Luke 24:35*

Because the Eucharist is the central place where Christian friendship is celebrated, a book on friendship would not be complete without directly linking friendship and the Eucharist. The Eucharist is at once the source and summit of Christian friendship shared in community.

It was at a meal that Jesus said that he had not called his followers to be his servants but his friends. It was also at a meal that the weary disciples Jesus had met on the road to Emmaus finally recognized him. And so it is with us. We share meals with our friends and, in that act of sharing, friendship grows strong. When we share meals we come to know and recognize our friends in ways that renew and deepen the bonds of friendship. What binds Eucharist and friendship together is the experience of *Presence*.

To understand the meaning of either friendship or of the Eucharist we must know and have experienced the meaning of *Presence*. We must have felt the *Presence* of another person. We must know a meaning of *Presence* that transcends time and space. We must reflect on the *Presence* in our lives of friends that are near and friends that are far. We must believe that friends and relatives who have died are present with us. We must grieve for a *Presence* now lost to us, whether through death or failed friendship.

The experience of *Presence* of which I speak is not something that just happens. The sense of *Presence* of a friend or loved one grows gradually and imperceptibly. It grows out of many moments shared. The experience of *Presence* grows out of picnics, banquets, and simple meals shared. It grows out of tears shared, out of darkness and fears shared. The experience of *Presence* grows out of laughter and tenderness shared. It grows out of happy childhood days and special times of family sharing. *Presence* means most when it is associated with those few people from whom we receive unconditional acceptance and love.

My own understanding of *Presence* took on a new meaning for me last May. I had left Boston to give a workshop at a conference being held at a resort in northern Wisconsin knowing that my mother was in a hospital in Spokane, Washington. Because the doctor had assured us that there was nothing serious, I decided that there was no need for me to go home at that time. I called my mother to talk with her just before I left the airport to fly to Wisconsin.

On the final day of the meeting at the resort I went down to a small gift shop in the lodge to find just the right card to send to my mother, and then returned to my room to write a note. As I sat at a desk looking out over a small pond and the surrounding woods, I felt as though my mother were there with me. Somehow I felt her profound sense of loneliness. My fantasy was of her looking out a hospital window, feeling lonely and afraid. I felt in her the fear she had often spoken about, of being dependent on someone else and of having to be cared for.

As I wrote that card to my mother, I felt as though I were speaking to her and she was there looking over my shoulder as my words took form on paper. I told her that I felt her loneliness and her sense of fear. I remembered how she had often told me that she was lonely for my father who died several years ago and that she wanted to be with him.

So overpowering was my sense of her presence that I mailed the card and went out for a walk in the woods, knowing that I could talk out loud with my mother there. As I walked along a trail in the woods, I experienced my mother telling me, more powerfully than in words I could hear, "Tell God that I don't want to be alone. Tell him that I am ready. Tell him that I want to go to your father."

I had a long talk with God that afternoon. With a sense of urgency I said to him, "God, you listen carefully to my mom. All her life she has done what you asked of her. Please, do this her way. You can't say 'No' to my mom. She has never said 'No' to you."

I returned to my room somewhat exhausted and overwhelmed by the awareness of my mother's presence there. That night I dreamed about her. Again, I saw her looking out that hospital window. Again, I felt her loneliness and saw the longing in her eyes.

The following morning I received a call telling me that my mother had died at 6:30 a.m. In spite of my tears, I wanted to shout, "Hooray for you, mom! God did it your way . . . Hooray for you, God! You listened to my mom."

My mother never received the card. Three weeks later it was returned to me. Written large across the envelope were the words EXPIRED . . . RETURN TO SENDER. Though the card was returned I know that my mother received my message. I know that she was with me as I walked the hills in northern Wisconsin. And I know that I was with her in the hospital that last afternoon.

In the months that have followed since my mother's

death I have struggled to establish with her the same kind of bonds that I have with my father. He is present to me in ways that I would not have believed possible at the time of his death. My relationship with him grows deeper with each passing year.

It is not yet this way with my mother. The sound of her voice and her infectious laughter still ring in my ears. She seems at once to be nearer to me in time and yet farther away from me than my father. My conversations with him are easier. I have grown accustomed to reaching across the reality of his death to a presence that transcends time and place. I will learn to do this with my mother, too, when I let go of her and am open to a new kind of relationship with her.

After my father's death I needed to know that he was with me. I found some important insights into the meaning of his presence in Viktor Frankl's book *Man's Search for Meaning*. With great tenderness Frankl speaks of the overriding sense he had of the presence of his wife during the time that he was in a Nazi concentration camp. He says:

> I did not know whether my wife was alive, and I had no means of finding out . . . but at that moment it ceased to matter. There was no need for me to know; nothing could touch the strength of my love, my thoughts and the image of my beloved. Had I known that my wife was dead, I think that I would still have given myself, undisturbed by that knowledge, to the contemplation of her image, and that my mental conversation with her would have been just as vivid and just as satisfying.[1]

Not only did Frankl's words help me to establish a new relationship with my father, they also helped me to deal with the time and distance that often separate me from friends. No friend is with me always. No friend is com-

[1] Viktor Frankl, *Man's Search for Meaning* (New York: Washington Square Press, 1963), pp. 60-61.

pletely present to me even when we are together. Friends, like other people we meet during the course of any week, are present to us in different ways and in varying degrees.

The people with whom I ride on the subway and those I pass as I walk to work are present to me to a lesser degree than are those in Symphony Hall when I attend a concert. The presence of those with whom I share the daily noon Eucharist is more important to me than are the people present in the theater when I attend a movie.

Human relationships have, by their very nature, built-in limitations. We are limited by both our own lack of self-knowledge and knowledge of a friend. We sometimes discover and verbalize our feelings with great difficulty. We often find it frightening to accept the feelings expressed by a friend. Because we grow in different ways and at different rates, we may feel threatened by our awareness that a friend is not present to us in the same way he or she once was.

Growing to an understanding of presence that is not dependent on our ability to touch or talk with a friend—like my efforts to reach beyond my mother's death and experience her ongoing friendship—requires not only a kind of personal discipline but also a willingness to let go of another. When I learn how to set my friends free, when I free myself of the tendency to clutch and cling to another, I will not only have crossed a major threshold in dealing with my own death and that of someone I love, but I will have found one of the deepest dimensions of friendship.

Through an effort that has taken several years I now experience bonds with my father that are a source of strength and life for me. I look to him for support and help in making decisions. I find in him the love and care that have always been a part of my life. I realize that he is a friend to me and that even death has never separated us.

Though I know this is and will be just as true with my mother, I also know that I have not yet transcended my own need for her physical presence. My relationship with my father gives me a kind of security in every other relationship that I have because I know that the love and strength that come to us only through the presence of friends do not depend on physical proximity. There is a quality about my love for my father now that touches every other relationship in my life. That same quality helps me to understand the words of Jesus:

> Still, I must tell you in truth:
> it is for your own good that I am going
> because unless I go,
> the Advocate will not come to you;
> but if I do go,
> I will send him to you. . . .
> But when the Spirit of truth comes
> he will lead you to the complete truth. . . .
> *John 16: 7,13*

My father and mother are with me now because we were involved in one another's lives for a long time. Each of my parents can say to me as Jesus said to his friends, ''When I die the spirit of my life will remain with you. After I am gone, you will remember me and you will understand my life more completely.''

Every person experiences the pain of leave-taking. This reluctance to leave his friends is best expressed in Jesus' ongoing presence in the Eucharist. The Eucharist was Jesus' way of not having to say goodbye to his friends.

Jesus handed over his Spirit to us in a way that makes his presence in the Eucharist unique. No one else has ever gone away and sent his spirit into the lives of friends in the forceful way that the Spirit of Jesus is with us. It is the presence of the Spirit of Jesus which helps me understand the presence of my deceased parents in my life now. Because of Jesus I understand their lives more fully now.

I know my father better now than I did while he was alive. I know that this will be true of my relationship with my mother and, someday, with each of my brothers and sisters. Because of all that we have shared, laughter and tears, work and vacations, joy and sadness, failure and dreams for new life, our lives are interwoven in ways no longer separable.

Among all the memories of happy times together none is more vivid than that of our Sunday family dinner. When the ten of us came to that table we shared life in ways more special and sacred than I could realize at the time. We were nourished not only by the food that we ate but also by the friendship that we shared. As we broke bread together at our family table we learned how to break the bread of our lives not only for each other but also for and with all the people we would meet during the week that followed. Because we loved one another our family meals had a significance greater than our family bonds. And, when we come together now to share family meals, my father and mother are present with us. Their spirit lives on in the life of each of their children. This would not be true had we not been involved in each other's lives, had we not loved one another, however imperfectly that love was manifested.

So it is with the presence of a friend. When we make demands on another person or are afraid of intimacy because of the demands that faithful friendship makes on us, we do not experience fully the presence of that person. Presence, like friendship, is self-involving. Unless I understand this, I will understand neither what the presence of Jesus in the Eucharist asks nor what it gives.

I was reminded of this several years ago when I was

attending a meeting. At the closing liturgy, just before the words of consecration, the priest who was celebrating with us said, ''My friends, Jesus will not be made present here simply by the words that I will say. His presence here depends also on what you bring here. He is present to each of us in a different way and only to the extent that we break the bread and share the cup of our lives as he did. He is present here only if he is present to our lives in other ways.''

So it is with friendship. It is not the easy words we say, nor is it the gifts we give that make us friends. Friendship invites us to share not only bread broken, but our brokenness. Friendship invites us to share not only wine poured into glasses, but our lives poured out. Friendship challenges us to take seriously the words of Jesus and to understand their meaning for our lives as we share life with friends:

> Then he took some bread, and when he had given thanks, broke it and gave it to them saying, ''This is my body which will be given for you; do this as a memorial of me.'' He did the same with the cup after supper, and said, ''This cup is the new covenant in my blood which will be poured out for you.''
>
> *Luke 22: 19-20*

We remember Jesus best when we are faithful to our lives and when we share in faithful friendship. This is our memorial to him, the memorial to which he calls us in each Eucharist.

We recognize Jesus in the breaking of the bread only if we look for him in all of the events of our lives. We find him in the breaking of the bread only if we continue to search for the meaning of faithful friendship.

The ways in which we are present to ourselves, to a friend, to a stranger, to loved ones who have died, and to Jesus in the Eucharist are connected. The meaning of presence is not separate realities as it applies to any of these relationships. Every relationship we have touches every other one. When our relationships are faithful and healthy, every person we meet is enriched by every other friendship. Every relationship is present to each of the others. When relationships are limiting and destructive, others are diminished by them. They are deprived of the goodness that exists when friends share life.

When Jesus meets his friends on the road to Emmaus they do not immediately recognize him. In telling him what has happened it is clear that they have missed the meaning of Jesus' life. While speaking of their prophet who has been put to death they reveal their own disappointed expectations of Jesus. In saying, "Our own hope had been that he would be the one to set Israel free," (Luke 24:21) they reveal their lack of understanding of what Jesus' presence among them had meant while he was with them. It is only later, in the breaking of the bread, that they recognize Jesus. It is only after Pentecost, when the Spirit of Jesus is unleashed among them, that they begin to understand not only the meaning of his presence in the Eucharist but of what his presence had meant when he was with them.

Just as the presence of Jesus during his life here demanded more than the easy acclaim of the crowds, so the presence of Jesus in the Eucharist demands of us that we be involved in sharing the life that is his heritage to us. He reminds us that we are called to live our lives as he lived his. When we reflect on the life of Jesus, when we try to live as he lived, our awareness of his presence with us deepens. With each insight we gain through prayer and self-reflection, we experience the presence of Jesus with us now, and we are more present to one another.

When I think of the values that were clear in the lived experience of my parents, when I seek to make these values my own, I grow closer to my father and mother. With every effort on my part to internalize in my life those qualities that I cherished in my parents, I live more as they did. Every relationship I have is influenced by the ongoing friendship that I have with my father and my mother. Reaching even across death is possible. Transcending my desire for the physical presence of two people that I love helps me understand that I not only can do this with friends but that I must if I am ever to understand fully the meaning of presence in friendship.

Each time I look for and find the meaning of Jesus' life in the Bread of Life, I also discover the meaning of all life. I recognize not only him but myself, my friends, my loved ones. I find and meet not only him but every person whose life touches mine in any significant way. I can do this because the Spirit of Jesus present in the Eucharist is a unique, life-giving and all-encompassing presence. It is a presence calling us to be friends.